GOD, LANGUAGE, AND SCRIPTURE

Foundations of Contemporary Interpretation

Moisés Silva, Series Editor

Volume 4

GOD, LANGUAGE, AND SCRIPTURE

READING THE BIBLE IN THE LIGHT OF GENERAL LINGUISTICS

Moisés Silva

ZondervanPublishingHouse

Grand Rapids, Michigan

A Division of HarperCollins*Publishers*

GOD, LANGUAGE, AND SCRIPTURE
Copyright © 1990 by Moisés Silva

Requests for information should be addressed to:
Zondervan Publishing House
Grand Rapids, Michigan 49530

Library of Congress Cataloging-in-Publication Data

Silva, Moisés
    God, language, and Scripture : reading the Bible in the light of
general linguistics / Moisés Silva.
       p.   cm. — (Foundations of contemporary interpretation ; v. 4)
    Includes bibliographical references.
    ISBN 0-310-40951-9
    1. Bible—Language, style.   2. Languages—Religious aspects.
  I. Title   II. Series
  BS537.B544   1990
  220.4—dc20 :90-33799

                                                    CIP

Edited by Gerard Terpstra
Designed by Louise Bauer

Printed in the United States of America

95 96 97 98 99 00 / DH / 10 9 8 7 6 5 4 3 2

A Tía Mecha

CONTENTS

PREFACE

One of the purposes of this book is to provide guidance in the use of the biblical languages. Unlike the other volumes in the *Foundations of Contemporary Interpretation* series, therefore, this one assumes some acquaintance with Greek and Hebrew. I should emphasize, however, that there is very little technical material here. Indeed, in the process of writing the book I found myself simplifying the subject matter more and more. Actual Greek and Hebrew scripts are used rarely, and the transliteration of Hebrew follows a very broad system (for example, no distinction is made on the basis of vowel "length"). Readers with any experience in consulting Bible commentaries should have little trouble following the argument even if they have not had formal training in the languages. (For the benefit of advanced readers, I have provided abundant bibliographical information in the footnotes.)

I have greatly enjoyed this opportunity to put down on paper ideas that had been brewing for more than two decades. Several generations of students, both at Westmont College and at Westminster Theological Seminary, have helped me develop those ideas. I am indebted to Richard J. Erickson (Fuller Theological Seminary) for serving as the formal reader of the manuscript. John Lübbe, Raymond B. Dillard, J. Alan Groves, and Vern S. Poythress, who also read a draft of the book, offered valuable suggestions and encouragement. I am also grateful to the administration and board of Westminster for granting me a study leave that made possible the production of the manuscript.

ABBREVIATIONS

BJRL	*Bulletin of the John Rylands Library*
BJS	Brown Judaic Studies
BRE	Biblioteca románica española
BT	*Bible Translator*
CBQ	*Catholic Biblical Quarterly*
CGNT	Cambridge Greek Testament Commentaries
CTL	Cambridge Textbooks in Linguistics
GKC	Gesenius-Kautzsch-Cowley, *Hebrew Grammar*
JETS	*Journal of the Evangelical Theological Society*
JSOTSS	Journal for the Study of the Old Testament Supplement Series
JTS	*Journal of Theological Studies*
LTCS	*Linguistics: The Cambridge Survey* (ed. Newmeyer, 1988)
NICNT	New International Commentary on the New Testament
NTS	*New Testament Studies*
SBLDS	Society of Biblical Literature Dissertation Series
SBLMS	Society of Biblical Literature Monograph Series
SBLSS	Society of Biblical Literature Semeia Studies
SBT	Studies in Biblical Theology
WBC	Word Biblical Commentary
WEC	Wycliffe Exegetical Commentary
WTJ	*Westminster Theological Journal*
WUNT	Wissenschaftliche Untersuchungen zum Neuen Testament

1
INTRODUCTION

It is approximately the year 2790. The most powerful
nation on earth occupies a large territory in Central Africa, and
its citizens speak Swahili. The United States and other English-
speaking countries have long ceased to exist, and much of the
literature prior to 2012 (the year of the Great Conflagration) is
not extant. Some archaeologists digging in the western regions
of North America discover a short but well-preserved text that
can confidently be dated to the last quarter of the twentieth
century. It reads thus:

> Marilyn, tired of her glamorous image, embarked on a new
> project. She would now cultivate her mind, sharpen her verbal
> skills, pay attention to standards of etiquette. Most important of
> all, she would devote herself to charitable causes. Accordingly,
> she offered her services at the local hospital, which needed
> volunteers to cheer up terminal patients, many of whom had
> been in considerable pain for a long time. The weeks flew by.
> One day she was sitting at the cafeteria when her supervisor
> approached her and said: "I didn't see you yesterday. What were
> you doing?" "I painted my apartment; it was my day off," she
> responded.

The archaeologists know just enough English to realize
that this fragment is a major literary find that deserves closer

inspection, so they rush the piece to one of the finest philologists in their home country. This scholar dedicates his next sabbatical to a thorough study of the text and decides to publish an exegetical commentary on it, as follows:

> We are unable to determine whether this text is an excerpt from a novel or from a historical biography. Almost surely, however, it was produced in a religious context, as is evident from the use of such words as *devoted, offered, charitable*. In any case, this passage illustrates the literary power of twentieth-century English, a language full of wonderful metaphors. The verb *embarked* calls to mind an ocean liner leaving for an adventuresome cruise, while *cultivate* possibly alerts the reader to Marilyn's botanical interests. In those days North Americans compared time to a bird—probably the eagle—that flies.
>
> The author of this piece, moreover, makes clever use of word associations. For example, the term *glamorous* is etymologically related to *grammar*, a concept no doubt reflected in the comment about Marilyn's "verbal skills." Consider also the subtleties implied by the statement that "her supervisor approached her." The verb *approach* has a rich usage. It may indicate a similar appearance or condition (*this painting approaches the quality of a Picasso*); it may have a sexual innuendo (*the rapist approached his victim*); it may reflect subservience (*he approached his boss for a raise*). The cognate noun can be used in contexts of engineering (e.g., access to a bridge), sports (of a golf stroke following the drive from the tee), and even war (a trench that protects troops besieging a fortress).
>
> Society in the twentieth century is greatly illumined by this text. The word *patient* (from *patience,* meaning "endurance") indicates that sick people then underwent a great deal of suffering: they endured not only the affliction of their physical illness, but also the mediocre skills of their medical doctors, and even (to judge from other contemporary documents) the burden of increasing financial costs.
>
> A few syntactical notes may be of interest to language students. The preposition *of* had different uses: causal (*tired of*), superlative (*most important of all*), and partitive (*many of whom*). The simple past tense had several aoristic functions: *embarked* clearly implies determination, while *offered* suggests Marilyn's once-for-all, definitive intention. Quite noticeable is the tense

variation at the end of the text. The supervisor in his question uses the imperfect tense, "were doing," perhaps suggesting monotony, slowness, or even laziness. Offended, Marilyn retorts with a punctiliar and emphatic aorist, "I painted."

Readers of Bible commentaries, as well as listeners of sermons, will recognize that my caricature is only mildly outrageous. What is wrong with such a commentary? It is not precisely that the "facts" are wrong (though even these are expressed in a way that misleads the reader). Nor is it sufficient to say that our imaginary scholar has taken things too far. There is a more fundamental error here: a misconception of how language normally works.

Our familiarity with the English language helps us see quite clearly that any "exegesis" such as the one I have just made up is, in the first place, an *overinterpretation* of the passage. Except perhaps in certain poetic contexts, we do not use words and grammatical functions as suggested by those comments. Of course, none of us—not even the finest scholar—can acquire the same familiarity with biblical Hebrew and New Testament Greek that we have with our native, living tongue. Consequently, it is a little easier to read alien concepts into an ancient text and sound quite scholarly as we do it. And if the text in question was written by a great classical author, we are even more readily disposed to assume that it contains great richness of meaning.

The problem intensifies when we deal with Scripture. Surely an inspired text must be full of meaning: we can hardly think that so much as a single word in the Bible is insignificant or dispensable. True enough. But we must never forget that God has spoken to us in the language of the people. Much of what passes for biblical interpretation, whether in books or sermons, implies that God has used an artificial, coded, or even esoteric language. Ironically, not a few examples of "grammatico-historical exegesis" suggest that the Bible is as distant from common believers as it was assumed by the proponents of the allegorical method. We must recall this basic principle: the richness and divine origin of the biblical *message* are not compromised by the naturalness and simplicity of the *form* in which God has chosen to communicate to us.

In addition to overinterpreting the passage, however, our whimsical commentary above is deficient at a more important level: it contributes virtually nothing to the reader's understanding of what the passage actually says! A simple translation into twenty-eighth-century Swahili would have conveyed far more accurately and efficiently the point of the text. Similarly, clear English versions of the Bible communicate to the modern reader the main (and therefore most important) point of any passage without recourse to obscure points of grammar.

Preachers who make appeals to "the original" may in some cases help their readers obtain a better insight into Scripture. More often than not, however, such appeals serve one of two functions: (1) they merely furnish illustrations to heighten interest so that hearers *think* they have a better understanding of the passage (cf. the comment on *embark* above); (2) they provide the occasion to make a point that has little to do with the passage (cf. the comment on *patient*).

In a Christian newspaper addressed specifically to preachers, the author of a column entitled "Gems from the Greek New Testament" focused on the noun *analysis* in 2 Timothy 4:6 ("the time of my *departure* is at hand"):

> The word which Paul chose to express his departure . . . from which our word analysis originates, is very unique and picturesque. . . . The beauty of this word is seen in the words from which it is formed: *ana* and *lusis*. The root of this word, *lusis*, was used extensively as a legal term to designate release from a binding obligation. An illustration of this is found in the release from a loan in a document dated 101 A.D. [The author proceeds to describe and quote the document.] As this example clearly illustrates, *lusis* indicates the release from a binding contract because the obligations of that contract were fulfilled. Another example of this meaning is found in the New Testament. In dealing with marriage, Paul writes, "Art thou bound to a wife? seek not to be loosed," *lusis* (I Cor. 7:27). Again, the idea expressed is the release from a legal obligation.

The preposition *ana*, which is attached to *lusis*, expresses the basic meaning of up. Even when it is attached to a word written in composition, it retains the idea of the direction up. . . . Examine this word within the context of Paul's usage. Paul was viewing his death as a release upward from his binding contract. The contract was the work which he was called to do. Furthermore, he was entitled to this release because he had fulfilled the obligations of the contract. . . . What a beautiful way to view death! The release from our binding, contractual obligations to God as a child of God. Most of us look forward to the day when the mortgage on our house is paid off. Should not we also look forward to the day when God releases us from our obligation to Him through death?[1]

Certain kinds of commentaries often fall into the same trap. But even the better ones may convey, by their excessive attention to linguistic detail, a false impression of the nature of language and thus fail to explain what the biblical author was actually seeking to communicate. I am not suggesting, of course, that detailed linguistic analysis of a text is in itself harmful or irrelevant. Indeed, much of this book is devoted to helping readers in that very task. But every facet of interpretation must be kept in proper perspective, and the more we know about the nature of language, the more likely we are to "handle correctly the word of God" (2 Tim. 2:15).

Unfortunately, language is one of those fields of study—like psychology—where experts abound. The reason is simple. All of us are continually exposed to human behavior (our own no less than that of others), of which language is one form Inevitably, and often unconsciously, we form judgments about behavior on the basis of our daily experience.

The cynics among my readers may well be thinking,

---

[1]This material appeared in *Pulpit Helps* 10, no. 12 (Sept. 1985): 1. One could just as easily focus on another meaning of the noun *solution* and argue that Paul has in mind the final resolution of all our earthly problems. The figurative meaning "to depart" for the cognate verb, *analyō*, probably arose from the nautical usage, "loose from moorings, weigh anchor." Someone may want to suggest that perhaps what Paul really intended was the picturesque notion of "sailing into the sunset"! Neither of these two suggestions is less probable than the meaning "release upward from a binding contract."

"Yes, and the narrower the scope of that experience, the more dogmatic are those judgments likely to be!" Naturally, if we notice a certain type of behavior more than once (or only once, for that matter), we do tend to generalize, to infer a rule or principle from that observation. It seldom occurs to us that, even if we have led an unusually rich life, our casual personal observations represent but a *minuscule* ("statistically insignificant") sample of a *haphazard* cross-section of human society.

But personal experience is a very powerful emotional factor that will stand up against reams of contrary evidence, as anyone who has tried to debunk "old wives' tales" must have found out. And the phenomenon of language, for some reason or another, can elicit very profound emotions indeed. People who write books on language, therefore, must be singularly ingenuous or have very little regard for their longevity. In either case, they deserve pity.

Also to be pitied, of course, are people who write books on biblical interpretation—perhaps the only subject that draws an even more passionate response than linguistic judgments. And so I have gleefully decided to write a book on the significance of language for biblical interpretation. Only if I have succeeded in drawing out your deepest sympathy, my reader, do I invite you to read on.

Just as responsible psychologists seek to avoid the shortcomings of personal observation by means of intensive and systematic research, usually supplemented by independent work done in the broader community of scholars, so it is with linguists. I use the term *linguist* not in its popular sense, "someone who knows many languages" (the more precise, though admittedly cacophonous, term *polyglot* better fills that slot), but in the professional sense. A linguist is not necessarily proficient in many languages, though a wide familiarity with linguistic groups certainly helps.[2]

The discipline of linguistics is often referred to as *modern*

---

[2]It is even conceivable (though in practice not very likely) that someone who has difficulties acquiring fluency in a foreign language could become fairly competent in various forms of linguistic research.

linguistics to indicate its relatively recent development. This fact may seem surprising, since language study can be traced back to the ancient world, but here precisely lies an important clue to what linguists do. While many of the ancient concerns still come under the purview of linguistics, a series of distinctive emphases set the modern discipline apart from the earlier periods. Another clue lies in the label *linguistic science*: it was not until the last decades of the nineteenth century that linguists were prepared to make claims of a scientific character (though there are some significant differences between twentieth-century linguists and even their immediate predecessors, as we will see).

Most helpful of all, however, is the term *general linguistics* (more or less synonymous with *modern linguistics*). In contrast to scholars who devote their lives to the study of a specific language, such as French grammar and literature, linguists pay primary attention to the understanding of languages generally. They too may, of course, have a special interest in French, but they will probably have gained some expertise in at least one language family not closely related to French. They will use their knowledge of a specific language to enhance their understanding of *language* as such; conversely, they may apply that general understanding to the study of a specific tongue.

What all this means for us is that the systematic data accumulated by linguists over many years can correct our personal, hit-or-miss impressions. God has in his wisdom spoken to us in the Bible through human languages (Hebrew, Aramaic, and Greek). If we ignore the character of human language, we will likely misunderstand Scripture. All languages make heavy use of imagery, for example. Forget that fact, and you will decide that David was not a person but a lamb ("The Lord is my shepherd"). But not every feature of language is so immediately obvious. This is where linguistics comes in.

2
BIBLICAL PERSPECTIVES
ON LANGUAGE

Before seeking to apply linguistic principles to biblical hermeneutics, we must attend to a major question: What does the Bible itself have to say about language? Surely anyone committed to the authority of Scripture will want an answer. After all, we cannot expect to solve differences of opinion about details without a broad, coherent framework. In other words, we require a foundational, conceptual context if we hope to evaluate linguistic theories and methods responsibly. But such a framework or meaningful context is beyond our reach unless we take God's revelation into account.[1]

[1]Not every Christian will agree with such an approach. My own views on this question have been influenced by Abraham Kuyper's discussion in a chapter entitled "The Twofold Development of Science," in *Principles of Sacred Theology* (Grand Rapids: Eerdmans, 1954; orig. 1898), § 48–51. Cf. also Cornelius Van Til, *A Christian Theory of Knowledge* (Phillipsburg, N.J.: Presbyterian and Reformed, 1969), pp. 36–37: "The facts of the universe in general may either be regarded in the light of the system of truth presented in Scripture or they may be seen in the light of some other system of truth that men think they possess. . . . In every discussion about every fact, therefore, it is the two principles, that of the believer in Scripture and that of the non-Christian, that stand over against one another. Both principles are totalitarian. Both claim all the facts. It is in the light of this point that the relation of the Bible as the infallible Word of God to the 'facts' of science and history must finally be understood." I hasten to add, however, that even Christians who belong to a

Moreover, the need for reflection on this issue is magnified by some apparent conflicts between the Bible and modern linguistics. What are the origins of human language? How did linguistic variation develop? Is oral communication of greater significance than written literature? Is there such a thing as a standard of linguistic "correctness"? It may well be, of course, that the Bible will not give us the kind of information we are looking for. Certainly we should not expect the Scriptures to provide a complete and well-defined philosophical framework for every intellectual discipline. On the other hand, the effort must be made to discover whether God has revealed basic principles that are applicable to our understanding of what language is and how it works.

LANGUAGE AND CREATION

In fact, Scripture has a great deal to say on the subject. We no sooner begin reading in Genesis than we are faced by the statement that "God said . . . ." It is a startling expression, since God does not have a physical body—and even if he did, why should speech have anything to do with the creation of the world? The ancient rabbis were not far from the truth when they suggested that this form of expression was intended to emphasize God's power: "The artist—he can make nothing at all except by hard work; but the Holy One, blessed be He—He makes things by the mere breath of a word."[2] God does not need to plan and prepare, to organize a labor force, to toil for an extended period of time. God needs only to utter the word, and

different theological tradition have more and more acknowledged the importance of subjecting every area of knowledge to the truths of Scripture. Witness in particular the growing number of Christian colleges that have sought to integrate their curriculum on the basis of the evangelical faith.

[2]*Midrash Tehillim* 18:26, from William G. Braude, trans., *The Midrash on Psalms*, 2 vols. (Yale Judaica Series 13; New Haven: Yale University Press, 1959), 1:257. In both Jewish and Samaritan thought, incidentally, one finds an association between the divine name, *YHWH*, and the creative word, *yehi*, "let there be." See Jarl E. Fossum, *The Name of God and the Angel of the Lord: Samaritan and Jewish Concepts of Intermediation and the Origin of Gnosticism* (WUNT 36; Tübingen: J. C. B. Mohr, 1985), pp. 76–84.

it is done: "Let them praise the name of the Lord, for he commanded and they were created" (Ps. 148:5).

We may wish to reflect further, however, on why this particular expression was used. Why not represent God as simply waving his hand, for example? Surely it is to call attention not only to God's power but specifically the power that is attached to his *word*. From the very beginning of the biblical narrative the power of God's word is impressed on the reader. The theme will recur often and at critical junctures in the succeeding biblical revelation. Moreover, it has often been noted that just as God exercises his divine sovereignty by his speaking (and by his naming [Gen. 1:5, 8]), so also Adam is represented as fulfilling God's mandate by naming the animals (Gen. 2:20). The connection between divine and human speech calls for careful thought, since it is part of the larger question about the creation of man, male and female, as the image of God. What is this image?

The extensive and heated theological debates that have arisen in answer to that question can be rather intimidating. Much of the discussion has been vitiated, however, by the tendency to phrase the question thus: What is the image of God *in* man? The Scriptures do not use that precise expression.[3] This concern may appear trivial or hair-splitting, yet the failure to

---

[3] I am indebted to my former teacher Norman Shepherd for help in clarifying this issue. (The subsequent comments on anthropomorphism also owe much to his lectures.) Claus Westermann, in *Genesis 1–11: A Commentary* (Minneapolis: Augsburg, 1984), p. 157, makes the valid point that the passage is concerned with "the nature of the act of creation which enables an event to take place between God and humans"; he creates a false dichotomy, however, when he deduces that the text is *not* concerned with the nature of human beings. A recent and helpful work on this topic is Philip Edgcumbe Hughes, *The True Image: The Origin and Destiny of Man in Christ* (Grand Rapids: Eerdmans and Leicester: Inter-Varsity, 1989), especially chaps. 1–2; note also the comprehensive volume by G. C. Berkouwer, *Man as the Image of God* (Grand Rapids: Eerdmans, 1962), and the fine article by D. J. A. Clines, "The Image of God in Man," *Tyndale Bulletin* 19 (1968): 53–103. For the history of interpretation see A.-G. Hamman, *L'homme, image de Dieu. Essai d'une anthropologie chrétienne dans l'église des cinq premiers siècles* (Relais-études 2; Paris: Desclée, 1987), and Gunnlaugur A. Jónsson, *The Image of God: Genesis 1:26–28 in a Century of Old Testament Research* (CB OT Series 26; [Lund:] Almqvists & Wiksell International, 1988).

ask the right question can be very misleading. As long as students try to identify the image of God *in* human beings, they will look for some entity (the soul? the spirit?) or quality (immortality? ability to worship?). But the text of Genesis does not encourage us to look for some specific item. Man *as a whole*, male and female, is described as being made in God's image.

It is perhaps an exaggeration, but not by much, to say that *every* aspect of human beings is a reflection of the divine image. More to the point, the total complex of those aspects is what constitutes the image. Our emotions, to be sure, have been corrupted by sin, but even such "negative" features as anger and jealousy derive originally from holy divine qualities. And although God does not possess a physical body, our bodies too reflect certain aspects of who God is.

> Take heed, you senseless ones among the people;
>   you fools, when will you become wise?
> Does he who implanted the ear not hear?
> Does he who formed the eye not see?

These rhetorical questions from Psalm 94:8–9 are striking in several respects. At the very least, they throw light on biblical *anthropomorphisms* (figurative descriptions that attribute human characteristics to God). The notion that God thereby accommodates to our imperfect human understanding contains an element of truth, to be sure, but perhaps we are approaching the issue from the wrong end. Our use of this term reflects our human-centered perspective. Indeed, it is not altogether far-fetched to say that descriptions of what *we* are and do should be termed "theomorphisms"!⁴ In other words, it is not as though God looks at our existence and searches for some quality that will illustrate in simple language who God is. Rather, our human qualities are themselves but a reflection of God's person and attributes. And so the tables must be turned. With regard to God's speech in particular, the real question is not "How can God speak (since he does not have a body)?" but "How can *we*

---

⁴This term can be misleading, however, especially if it suggests that the humanlike descriptions of God should be taken literally rather than metaphorically. Hughes rightly argues against this conception (*The True Image*, p. 12).

speak?" The answer to this is: We are made in the image of a God who speaks.[5]

We conclude, then, that when Genesis tells us that God created Adam and Eve "in his own image," the focus is not on some specific quality but on human beings in their totality. We can hardly refrain from asking, however, whether certain human characteristics, more than others, are indicative of this truth. After all, animals too have eyes and ears. Just how are we different from animals? Many legitimate answers could be given, such as in our ability to walk erect, to use tools, to commune with God. But if we are interested in what the author of Genesis had in mind, we should inquire whether the context gives us any clues.

Indeed it does, for Genesis 1:26 explicitly connects the concept of image with that of dominion: "Let us make man in our image, in our likeness, *and let them rule* . . . ." We probably should not infer, as some have done, that image simply equals dominion. The connection between the two concepts appears to be rather that the one serves as the basis for the other.[6] God made Adam and Eve like him and so they are able to exercise dominion over the earth. Of course, insofar as they do exercise

---

[5]This line of thought, incidentally, can and should be carried in other directions. For example, Geerhardus Vos argued persuasively that Jesus' parables, insofar as they appeal to nature, should not be considered mere illustrations used because they are convenient and simple to understand. Rather, we may say that spiritual truths are built into the very structure of the world God has created. See Vos' *Biblical Theology: Old and New Testaments* (Grand Rapids: Eerdmans, 1948), p. 380.

[6]Cf. Franz Delitzsch, *A New Commentary on Genesis*, 2 vols. (Edinburgh: T. & T. Clark, 1899), 1:100: the rule promised is not a reference to the content of the image "but its consequence, or, as Frank thinks it better to express it . . . not its nature, but the manifestation of that nature." This interpretation can be supported, though not conclusively proved, from the grammar: the word *and* translates the so-called "weak *waw*," which is often used after cohortatives to indicate purpose. Cf. Gordon J. Wenham, *Genesis 1–15* (WBC 1; Waco, Tex.: Word, 1987), p. 4, with reference to GKC §109f. Note also S. R. Driver, *A Treatise on the Use of the Tenses in Hebrew*, 3d ed. (Oxford: Clarendon, 1969; orig. 1912), chap. 5, and most recently Bruce K. Waltke and M. O'Connor, *An Introduction to Biblical Hebrew Syntax* (Winona Lake, Ind.: Eisenbrauns, 1990) §39.2.5.

that dominion they may be regarded as vice-regents under God, so that their ruling function too derives from, *and is like,* God's reign over his creation. Just as God created the world (chap. 1), so Adam tills the land (2:15). Thus one clear respect in which human beings are different from animals is that humans cultivate the ground. And agriculture may certainly be viewed as but one specific expression of a much broader set of activities (all work in general, cultural functions, etc.) that reflect the rule of Adam and Eve and their descendants.

But there is more. As indicated earlier, Genesis 1–2 focuses on one specific analogy between God and Adam: both of them speak and both use speech to exercise rule. The biblical text, then, encourages us to view language as a distinctive human quality, as a particularly clear manifestation of the divine image. The fact is that we talk . . . and talk and talk incessantly. And as we look around at creation we find that we are the only ones that do![7]

Not surprisingly, scholars from a wide variety of perspectives have commented on the uniqueness of language. Ray Past,

---

[7]This is not to deny that communication of one sort or another goes on among animals. Nor do I wish to contest the claim that chimpanzees, for example, can be taught to use some elementary forms of communication that resemble human language. But the most successful experiments to date serve, if anything, to emphasize the enormous difference between the "language" of the most intelligent animals—even after extensive training—and the linguistic competence of even a three-year old human being. Note the fine synthesis by Richard A. Demers, "Linguistics and Animal Communication," *LTCS* 3:314–35, especially p. 333: "Recent research has certainly shown that the primates have communication systems which are more elaborate than was assumed earlier. What all nonhuman communication systems lack, however, is the unboundedness in scope that is the central feature of human language. The structural properties of the cotton-top tamarin's . . . appear to be similar to the lower levels of the structural properties of human language. . . . At the level of both word and phrase, however, human language achieves an openness and productivity totally beyond the capability of any nonhuman communication system." (For a more positive, but still cautious, evaluation in the same volume, see William Orr Dingwall, "The Evolution of Human Communicative Behavior," *LTCS* 3:274–313, especially pp. 289–90.) At any rate, the main and rather simple point that I wish to make is that speech is obviously *not* something that characterizes the animal world.

for example, remarks that "whatever the theologians may have to say, the most *obvious* thing distinguishing men and women from what we like to call lower forms of life is *speech*." The well-known sociobiologist Edward O. Wilson, from a non-Christian, evolutionist perspective, argues as follows: "All of man's unique social behavior pivots on his use of language, which is itself unique. . . . The development of human speech represents a quantum jump in evolution comparable to the assembly of the eucaryotic cell." And Noam Chomsky, arguably the most influential linguist of our generation, puts it this way: "When we study human language, we are approaching what some might call the 'human essence,' the distinctive qualities of mind that are, so far as we know, unique to man."[8]

Chomsky's remark, in particular, calls attention to the highly debated issue concerning the relation between language and thought. Is thought possible without language? The answer, of course, depends largely on how we define thought. No doubt in some sense even dogs and cats "think," if all we have in view is a set of mental processes (such as recognition) related to the animals' behavior. Again, we may want to argue that babies, before they learn to speak, engage in some form of thought.

Normally, however, we use the term *thought* to indicate a rational capacity characteristic of older children and adults— and this kind of thinking always appears to function alongside language. (Deafness and muteness, incidentally, do not prevent the development of linguistic skills. Sign language, for example, is indeed a language.) The question whether thought is possible without language is theoretically interesting, but it has little practical relevance. As far as we can tell, all of the thinking that in fact goes on is inextricably tied to linguistic competence.

Adam's naming the animals, therefore, is not a mere historical curiosity, nor does it reflect some kind of primitive mythology. The point is that Adam cannot rule the earth unless

[8]Ray Past, *Language as a Lively Art* (Dubuque, Iowa: William C. Brown, 1970), p. 1. Edward O. Wilson, *Sociobiology: The New Synthesis* (Cambridge, Mass.: Belknap, 1975), pp. 555–56. Noam Chomsky, *Language and Mind*, enlarged ed. (New York: Harcourt Brace Jovanovich, 1972), p. 1.

he understands it, that his understanding is bound to the need for ordering what he sees, and that such ordering takes place through language.[9] While we should avoid extreme claims, such as the view that we create the world with our language,[10] most of us underestimate the power of language to bring order to our minds. The toddler's constant "What is that?" is more than childish curiosity. Similarly, the amateur collector of butterflies and the lover of classical music—indeed anyone interested in anything—will feel that they have failed to master their field unless they have names for everything.

In sum, the biblical narrative presents human language not precisely as a gift created by God for Adam but as a powerful attribute that is (1) intrinsic to God's own being and activity, (2) clear evidence of the fact that Adam and Eve were distinctive creatures made in God's image, and (3) inseparable from the mandate to Adam and Eve to rule creation.

LANGUAGE AND SIN

The entrance of sin into the world immediately affected the role for which Adam and Eve were created. They continued to bear the image of their Creator, but not with the same glory. Their rule over creation now involved frustration and pain. Language was now used to evade responsibility (Gen. 3:12–13),

---

[9]For the view that naming in the Bible is little more than an act of discernment, see George W. Ramsey, "Is Name-Giving an Act of Domination in Genesis 2:23 and Elsewhere?" *CBQ* 50 (1988): 24–35. Much of Ramsey's material is valuable, but are we to say that God's own naming (1:5, 8) simply reflects God's discernment?

[10]It is often difficult to determine whether writers who make those claims are using only figurative expressions. At least some of them appear to mean what they say quite literally (and certainly the Kantian doctrine of reason is no mere metaphor). Linguists, psychologists, anthropologists, and philosophers continue to debate to what extent our thought is bound by our language. Although we can hardly doubt that our language *predisposes* us to think in certain ways, no one has been able to prove that we are unable to overcome the resultant limitations. For an up-to-date and insightful survey of the debate on linguistic determinism/relativity, see Jane H. Hill, "Language, Culture, and World View," *LTCS* 4:14–36.

to aid murder (4:6), and to challenge God's sovereignty (4:23–24). Some of the effects of sin on human speech deserve special attention.

The Confusion of Tongues

The story of the Tower of Babel (Gen. 11:1–9) stands as one of the most carefully crafted pieces of narrative in the Book of Genesis.[11] The passage naturally divides into two balanced sections, the first announcing what man proposed (vv. 1–4), the second declaring what God disposed (vv. 5–9). The contrast between the two sections is heightened by mockery. In place of stone and mortar, fragile brick with tar was used by these wicked and foolish people (v. 3). Their summons, "Come, let us build" (v. 4), is echoed in God's response, "Come, let us go down" (v. 7). They desired a great name, but the name their city received—which sounds like the Hebrew word for "confusion," *babel*—was laughable. Their grand purpose was protection lest they be scattered over the earth, yet "the Lord scattered them over the face of the whole earth" (vv. 8–9). An Israelite listening to the story would have smiled with amusement from the very point where the wicked men begin to speak, since the choice of words with a high frequency of the consonants *b* and *l* (*habba nilbenah lebanim*, "Come, let's make bricks" [v. 3]) anticipates the end of their designs.

But what is the point of the story? Is this one among the similar myths in a variety of ancient cultures intended to explain the origin of linguistic diversity?[12]

When we consider how much the Book of Genesis does *not* tell us about the origin and development of civilization, it seems doubtful that this passage was written for the purpose of satisfying historical curiosity. In any case, we can demonstrate

---

[11]For much of what follows I am indebted to Umberto Cassuto's remarkable work, *A Commentary on the Book of Genesis*, 2 vols. (Jerusalem: Magnes, 1961–64, orig. 1944–49) 2:225–49.

[12]It is commonplace for modern commentators to refer to this passage as *etiological* in character, that is, motivated by a desire to elucidate the causes of present realities. Cf. Westermann, *Genesis 1–11*, pp. 534–35, 553–54.

that over the course of time languages will naturally diversify (perhaps the clearest example is the development of the Romance languages, such as French and Spanish, from Latin), so this passage cannot explain every instance of language variation. It may well be that such an event as is described here could account for the origin of language *families* (such as the difference between the Indo-European family and the Afro-Asiatic family) and that a memory of the event is reflected in similar stories around the world. But the truth is that we do not have enough information to establish a clear correspondence between the event described in this passage and what we know of prehistoric language development. Moreover, we should not assume that language diversity *as such* is necessarily a bad thing or a reflection of God's curse.

Let us bear in mind that this passage serves as a backdrop to the call of Abraham. The Genesis narrative never loses sight of God's intention to save mankind (3:16). Some have argued that even the expulsion of Adam and Eve from the Garden of Eden was intended not only as a punishment but also as a means of aiding God's redemptive purposes.[13] Certainly the Flood, colossal as it was in its retributive power, preserved mankind from the total extinction toward which it was headed through sin. Similarly, when God says in 11:6, "If as one people speaking the same language they have begun to do this, then nothing they plan to do will be impossible for them," we may infer that the judgment on the tower and its builders was not void of grace. Indeed, the scattering of people over the face of the earth restrains them from fulfilling their evil intents.[14] Henceforth God focuses his redemptive work on Abraham and

---

[13]Although it is somewhat speculative, the point is that Adam and Eve, if allowed to eat of the tree of life in their state of disobedience, would have been *confirmed* for ever in that state and thus would have placed themselves outside the possibility of salvation.

[14]Cf. Westermann, *Genesis 1–11*, p. 551: success in building the tower "must lead to the absolute autonomy of humankind. Hence the limitation which belongs to their created state would be called into question. . . . Humanity exists only in its state as creature; so its continuation is endangered by the threat of autonomy."

his descendants, but the patriarch is told that the divine purposes are universal: ". . . and *all the peoples* on earth will be blessed through you" (12:3).

Evil Speech

The confusion resulting from the destruction of Babel implies more than our inability to understand languages foreign to us. That inability, no doubt, has often led to serious quarrels among nations and ethnic groups. But the multiplicity of languages throughout the world is perhaps only the reflection of a more fundamental discordant streak in humanity. After all, nations that speak the same language have hardly been invulnerable to the horrors of war! Without minimizing the role played by *substantive* differences of opinion among people, one must wonder how often we delude ourselves into thinking that our disputes have vital significance when in fact we have only failed to communicate clearly.[15]

It is difficult to say whether Genesis 11 alludes to this more general problem of human misunderstanding. Certainly there is nothing in the passage that appears to address the issue directly. I find it improbable, however, that a Hebrew audience, familiar with the rest of the Old Testament, would fail to link this story with the numerous scriptural warnings about the evils of the tongue.

Foremost among them are the severe commandments against harming our neighbor through deceitful words. Not only does the ninth commandment forbid giving false witness against our neighbors (Exod. 20:16); other passages in the

---

[15]Some decades ago, concern for the way in which the misuse of language harms human relationships led to the development of a movement known as General Semantics, made especially popular by S. I. Hayakawa et al., *Language in Thought and Action*, 4th ed. (New York: Harcourt Brace Jovanovich, 1978). Although it may be overly optimistic to think that defining our terms clearly is the key to solving many of our social and international problems, it seems undeniable that language manipulation—whether conscious or unconscious—and lack of proper communication (resulting from blindness to the other person's point of view) are prime sources of human conflict.

Pentateuch also emphasize and expand on this prohibition. "Do not spread false reports. Do not help a wicked man by being a malicious witness. . . . Have nothing to do with a false charge" (23:1, 7). The code in Leviticus 19 includes the following: "Do not lie. Do not deceive one another. . . . Do not curse the deaf. . . . Do not go about spreading slander among your people" (vv. 11, 14, 16). If a malicious witness is proven to have lied, "giving false testimony against his brother, then [the community must] do to him as he intended to do to his brother. You must purge the evil from among you" (Deut. 18:18–19).

Behind these strong precepts is the conviction that there is real power in speech.[16] Naïve Jack may have thought that words couldn't hurt him, but the wisdom teachers of Israel viewed slander and verbal abuse as far more damaging than sticks and stones. "With his mouth the godless destroys his neighbor"; "Reckless words pierce like a sword"; "Like a club or a sword or a sharp arrow is the man who gives false testimony against his neighbor" (Prov. 11:9; 12:18; 25:18). The Book of Psalms, which abounds with depictions of evil men, characteristically focuses on their speech. Not surprisingly, the apostle Paul supports his doctrine of the universality of sin by quoting, among others, three Psalms that condemn evil speaking: "Their throats are open graves; their tongues practice deceit"; "The poison of vipers is on their lips"; "Their mouths are full of cursing and bitterness" (Pss. 5:9; 140:3; 10:7; cited in Rom. 3:13–14).

Paul elsewhere enjoins believers not to misuse speech. Especially powerful is a series of commands in Ephesians 4:25–5:4:

> Therefore each of you must put off falsehood and speak truthfully to his neighbor. . . . Do not let any unwholesome talk come out of your mouths, but only what is helpful for building others up according to their needs. . . . Get rid of all bitterness,

---

[16]My use of the term *power* has nothing to do with magic or superstition. Anthony C. Thiselton has adequately dealt with this misconception in his article "The Supposed Power of Words in the Biblical Writings," *JTS* n.s. 25 (1974) 283–99. On the other hand, Thiselton's article, because of its polemical focus, is necessarily one-sided. The passages quoted below must be taken seriously.

rage and anger, brawling and slander, along with every form of malice. . . . Nor should there be obscenity, foolish talk or coarse joking, which are out of place, but rather thanksgiving.

But the apostle is not the only New Testament writer to show deep concern over this problem. The Gospel of Matthew records these strong words of our Lord against the Pharisees who blasphemed him: "You brood of vipers, how can you who are evil say anything good? For out of the heart the mouth speaks. . . . But I tell you that men will have to give account on the day of judgment for every careless word they have spoken" (Matt. 12:34, 36). Peter commands his readers to rid themselves "of all malice and all deceit, hypocrisy, envy, and slander of every kind"; he also enjoins them not to repay insult with insult and appeals to Psalm 34:12–16: "Whoever would love life and see good days must keep his tongue from evil and his lips from deceitful speech" (1 Peter 2:1; 3:10).

No writer is more forceful, however, than James. Early in his letter he advises us to be "slow to speak" (1:19); he reminds us that keeping the royal law includes proper speaking as well as acting (2:8, 12); he specifically condemns slander (4:11); and he recalls the Lord's command that our yes must be yes and our no must be no (5:12). In addition, he devotes a central section of his letter to a discussion of the restless and almost uncontrollable evil of the tongue (3:1–12). James seems to reflect the Old Testament conviction that, since our speech is tainted with sin, the more we speak the more we are likely to sin: "When words are many, sin is not absent" (Prov. 10:19; cf. v. 14; 17:27–28). Those who teach, therefore, take on an additional risk by the influence and authority they wield. They must learn to bridle their tongue, which controls their lives as a small rudder steers a large ship; then they will be "able to keep [their] whole body in check" (James 3:2, 4).

The verses I have cited in this section constitute but a fraction of the numerous biblical passages that emphasize the sinfulness of human speech. They are enough, however, to establish a vital truth. The Fall distorted, though it did not utterly destroy, the divine image borne by mankind. As God's image-bearers, we still speak, and our speech still has power to exercise dominion. But this power has been profaned, and sinners rule under the Prince of Darkness. Just as language is a uniquely clear reflection of the divine image, by the same token language has become a singularly blatant instrument of rebellion against the Creator.

LANGUAGE AND REDEMPTION

God's Word

The word through which God created a world that was "very good" (Gen. 1:31) must now become the instrument whereby he both judges a corrupted world and re-creates it for his glory. The word of judgment already appears in Eden, where God curses Satan and the ground and decrees pain and suffering for Adam and Eve (3:14–17). The destruction caused by the Flood is likewise attributed to God's word: "But at your rebuke the waters fled, at the sound of your thunder they took to flight" (Ps. 104:7).

The imagery of God's speaking through "natural" disasters is especially prominent in Psalm 29:

> The voice of the Lord is over the waters;
>   The God of glory thunders,
>   The Lord thunders over the mighty waters. . . .
> The voice of the Lord strikes
>   with flashes of lightning.
> The voice of the Lord shakes the desert;
>   the Lord shakes the Desert of Kadesh.
> The voice of the Lord twists the oaks
>   and strips the forests bare.

Similarly Jeremiah, as he denounces the false prophets, compares God's word with fire and with "a hammer that breaks a rock in pieces" (Jer. 23:29). Whereas God's breath was the source of life for mankind at the creation (Gen. 2:7), it has now become a scorching wind by which the very foundations of the earth are laid bare (Exod. 15:10; 2 Sam. 22:8–16; Isa. 11:15). Indeed, God's "tongue is a consuming fire," his voice "will shatter Assyria," and his breath is "like a stream of burning sulfur" (Isa. 30:27, 31, 33). And the New Testament assures us that "by the same word the present heavens and earth are reserved for fire, being kept for the day of judgment and destruction of ungodly men" (2 Peter 3:7).

Alongside the word of judgment, however, God utters the word of salvation. It is not absent even in Eden, where God tells the serpent that the seed of the woman will crush its head (Gen. 3:15). It becomes explicit in the word of promise to Abraham (12:2–3) and in precepts that bring prosperity (Lev. 18:5; Josh. 1:7; Ps. 1:2–3). Over and over again God speaks to his people a law that "is perfect, reviving the soul"; commands that "are radiant, giving light to the eyes"; and ordinances that "are sure and altogether righteous," indeed "more precious than gold" and sweeter "than honey from the comb" (Ps. 19:7–10).

Some will object that human language, being an imperfect medium, cannot convey a perfect divine message. It may well be true that no human language can express God's truth in exhaustive and precise detail, but that is far from conceding that divine truth is incommunicable to men and women. To admit that human beings are fallible is not to imply that human beings cannot utter true sentences. The statement "John F. Kennedy was assassinated in the early 1960s," though uttered by a fallible person through the imperfect medium of the English language, does not contain error. It may indeed lack in precision, but it is reliable. Similarly, that God should choose to communicate his revelation to us through the limited resources of human speech (the only way we will understand it) hardly indicates a faulty or fallible revelation.[17]

Let us keep in mind, however, that there is more to God's word than the communication of truth. For example, the power of God's word to preserve those who belong to him is brought home to the Israelites when they are told that God fed them

---

[17]See especially John M. Frame, "God and Biblical Language: Transcendence and Immanence," in God's Inerrant Word: An International Symposium on the Trustworthiness of Scripture, ed. J. W. Montgomery (Minneapolis: Bethany Fellowship, 1974), pp. 159–77.

"with manna, which neither you nor your fathers had known, to teach you that man does not live on bread alone but on every word that comes from the mouth of the LORD" (Deut. 8:3). At first blush this statement seems odd. If God wants to teach them that they cannot live by bread alone, why does he do it by giving them bread (i.e., manna)! Clearly, the contrast being made here is not—or at least not primarily—between physical sustenance (bread) and "spiritual" instruction (word), for part of what God's word does is to give the Israelites *physical* sustenance. The contrast is rather between self-reliance and dependence on God's power, between "natural" means and "supernatural" sustenance. In other words, what is being challenged here is the presumption that we can get along reasonably well with our own efforts and schemes. God had to humble the Israelites and let them come to the end of their rope so that they would recognize how dependent they were on the power of God's word for all their needs, physical or not.

The prophet Isaiah stresses the efficacy of God's word for salvation in a well-known passage where sinners are invited to "seek the Lord while he may be found" (Isa. 55:6–11). At times it may appear that the divine revelation is impotent, but we must not fool ourselves:

> As the rain and the snow
>   come down from heaven,
> and do not return to it
>   without watering the earth
> and making it bud and flourish,
>   so that it yields seed for the sower and bread
> for the eater,
>   so is my word that goes out from my mouth:
> It will not return to me empty,
>   but will accomplish what I desire
>   and achieve the purpose for which I sent it.

And the prophet Ezekiel prevents us from thinking that God's breath is only a destructive wind. Against the hopeless sight of a valley full of dry bones that have no life in them, the Lord commands:

"Prophesy to the breath; prophesy, son of man, and say to it, 'This is what the Sovereign LORD says: Come from the four winds, O breath, and breathe into these slain, that they may live.' " So I prophesied as he commanded me, and breath entered them; they came to life and stood up on their feet—a vast army. (Ezek. 37:9–10)

The Lord goes on to explain that this vision refers to the spiritual restoration of his people, which will be accomplished when he puts his Spirit in them (v. 14).[18]

God's Written Word

God's word is often described as coming to people orally; with reference to Abraham, for example, we are told that "the LORD appeared to him and said . . ." (Gen. 17:1). Moreover, the prophets as God's spokesmen openly proclaimed the revelation they received. But what happens to the message after the initial proclamation? Oral transmission is usually quite unstable, as all of us have learned when seeking to communicate through more than one intermediary! Something is necessary to insure the permanence of the message among God's people, and this is where *inscripturation* comes in.

The very idea is offensive to many people today who believe that "inscripturated revelation" is a contradiction in terms and an outrage against true religion—after all, how can God be circumscribed within a book? Such a conception, they will argue, can only suffocate faith to the point of extinction. The fact is, however, that God is said to have commanded Moses to write in certain key situations. After the defeat of the Amalekites at Rephidim, for instance, the Lord instructs him: "Write this on a scroll *as something to be remembered* and make sure that Joshua hears it, because I will completely erase the memory of the Amalekites from under heaven" (Exod. 17:14, my emphasis). Moreover, at the point where the Israelites are constituted a nation, God himself is represented as writing the

---

[18]In this passage, the words *Spirit, breath,* and *wind* are all renderings of the same Hebrew word, *ruaḥ.*

covenant with his own finger (Exod. 24:12; 31:18; 32:15–16; 34:1). The books of Deuteronomy and Joshua abound with references to the covenant that clearly focus attention on its written form (e.g., Deut. 28:58; 29:20; 30:10; Josh. 1:8; 8:31).[19]

The oft-heard advice, when dealing with potentially legal questions, to "put it down in writing" does not merely reflect a modern obsession. One of Isaiah's oracles includes the following: "Go now, write it on a tablet for them, inscribe it on a scroll, that for the days to come it may be an everlasting witness" (Isa. 30:8). The particular and important role played by the written word also lies behind God's explicit instructions to Jeremiah: "Write in a book all the words I have spoken to you"—a command that is linked to the Lord's promise of future redemption (Jer. 30:2–3). Similarly, Habakkuk is told: "Write down the revelation and make it plain on tablets so that a herald may run with it" (Hab. 2:2).

Very instructive in this regard is the perspective of the New Testament apostles, who saw themselves as communicating the very word of God (1 Thess. 2:13). While recognizing certain advantages in being able to speak face to face (cf. 2 John 12), they saw their writings as both useful and necessary when they themselves were absent (2 Cor. 13:10; 1 Tim. 3:14–15; 1 John 1:4; 2:12–14; Jude 3). Naturally, their inevitable death rendered such writings essential in preserving the foundational apostolic message (2 Peter 1:12–15; 3:1–2).[20] Appropriately,

---

[19]James Barr argues that this concern with written Scripture was only a late development in the Old Testament. Then, on the basis of the fact that Jesus does not appear to have written anything (plus other similar evidence), Barr makes the remarkable, indeed baffling, comment that in the Jewish culture of the day "committal to writing was an *unworthy* mode of transmission of the profoundest truth." See his book, *Holy Scripture: Canon, Authority, Criticism* (Philadelphia: Westminster, 1983), p. 12.

[20]As the old Latin proverb puts it, *Verba volant, scripta manent* ("What is spoken flies away, what is written remains"). From a strictly "secular" perspective, note the comment by Gillian Brown and George Yule, *Discourse Analysis* (CTL; Cambridge: Cambridge University Press, 1983), p. 14: "The major differences between speech and writing derive from the fact that one is essentially transitory and the other is designed to be permanent. It is exactly this point which D. J. Enright makes in the observation that 'Plato may once have

the last book of the Bible is characterized by repeated instructions for John to write what he saw (Rev. 1:11, 19; 2:1 et al.; 14:13; 19:9; 21:5).

As if to anticipate the modern objection to inscripturated revelation, Paul in 2 Timothy 3:16 explicitly identifies the *written* word (*graphē*) with God's very breath (*theopneustos*, "God-breathed"). In this striking turn of expression the New Testament encapsulates the whole range of Old Testament teaching concerning the life-giving power of God's word. If fallen humanity is to be redeemed, it will be only by means of that word, which once created and must now re-create.

God's Incarnate Word

That last statement should remind us, however, that God's word is not an impersonal force. Just as God was personally present in the creation of the world, so did he become personally present in the accomplishment of redemption. It was not simply a poetic strain that led the apostle John to begin his gospel by describing Jesus as *the Word*. That Word was there at the beginning of creation with God—indeed, that Word was God himself, and all things were created by him (John 1:1–3; cf. also Col. 1:16–17; Heb. 1:2–3).[21]

Moreover, he took up residence in our midst, because as the Word he is the Revealer of divine glory (John 1:14), and as the Son only he can make the Father known (John 1:18). After all, "no one knows the Father except the Son and those to whom the Son chooses to reveal him" (Matt. 11:27). It is that status and power that give Jesus the right to extend a unique invitation: "Come to me, all you who are weary and burdened, and I will give you rest" (Matt. 11:28).

We should mark, incidentally, that to recognize the Son of

---

thought more highly of speech than of writing, but I doubt he does now!' (Review in *The Sunday Times*, 24 January 1982)." Cf. also below, chap. 3, pp. 49–50.

[21]The last two references stress the continuing providential work of Christ in preserving the world he created, and Hebrews 1:3 in particular describes that work as something that takes place through "his powerful word."

God as the Word is not to minimize his *words*. It is sometimes argued that what really matters in our relationship with God is the *personal* element rather than the *propositional* and that, consequently, when evangelicals insist that revelation conveys information—and infallible information, no less—they are not only misconstruing the nature of revelation, they are also committing "bibliolatry" by putting the Bible where God alone belongs (as it is sometimes stated, they have replaced a human pope with a paper pope!).

Now this charge of "bibliolatry," in spite of its popularity, is really quite disconcerting. Imagine a ten-year-old who, after disobeying a parental instruction and having been scolded for it, defends herself as follows:

> Why are you scolding me? I am not being disobedient or disrespectful. Quite the contrary. I hold you in the highest esteem and am fully submissive to your authority. And just because of that I must regard your words as having only *derived* authority. Surely you would not want me to debase my commitment to you by elevating what is merely propositional to the level of the personal, would you? Indeed, hardly anything would be more offensive to your character than such an indiscriminate subservience to mere words.

Granted, this particular child is unusually precocious. But her logic approximates that of modern theologians who tell us that we should be submissive to God *rather than* to his words. Such a dichotomy between a person's authority and the authority of what that person says is both false and meaningless. It probably would not sit very well in the armed forces, either.[22] And certainly the very John who stressed the personal character of the Word knew nothing of such a distinction, since he reports Jesus as saying: "I tell you the truth, whoever hears my word

---

[22]Since this dichotomy approaches absurdity, I assume that the theologians in question are bothered not so much by the principle that a person's authority is bound in the authority of his or her words but rather by the view that the words of the Bible can in fact be identified as God's words. But modern theologians are not always straightforward in identifying clearly the object of their dislike. If they were, it might become all too obvious how distant is their religious frame of reference from that of the biblical writers.

and believes him who sent me has eternal life"; "Why is my language not clear to you? Because you are unable to hear what I say [*lit.* to hear my word]" (John 5:24; 8:43; and many other passages). The psalmists, for their part, seemed quite unconcerned about the charge of bibliolatry: "In God, whose word I praise, in God I trust" (Ps. 56:4; cf. v. 10; 68:4); "You have exalted above all things your name and your word" (Ps. 138:2).

Redeemed Speech

Earlier we saw a number of biblical passages that condemn evil speech; by implication, and in certain cases quite explicitly, these passages enjoin a radical change in the speech habits of those who have been redeemed through faith in Christ, the Word. Precisely because language is powerful, it must be used to build up rather than to destroy. Contemporary psychology has recognized the strong impact that positive words can have on the emotional health of children and even adults. The Book of Proverbs anticipated that insight: "The tongue of the righteous is choice silver. . . . The lips of the righteous nourish many"; "The words of the wicked lie in wait for blood, but the speech of the upright rescues them"; "From the fruit of his lips a man is filled with good things as surely as the work of his hands rewards him"; ". . . the tongue of the wise brings healing"; "A gentle answer turns away wrath" (Prov. 10:20–21; 12:6, 14, 19; 15:1).

The emphasis of Scripture on the right use of speech would seem to have a bearing also on current concerns about the supposed decay of English (and other modern languages). As we will have occasion to see in a later chapter, some of these concerns are not founded on a proper understanding of language. Many of the alleged corruptions in contemporary English reflect natural linguistic development and are found in other languages otherwise regarded as "superior" by these same critics (e.g., double-negative constructions are common in Ancient Greek). All the same, carelessness in our use of words *is* a legitimate concern, one to which Christians in particular should pay close attention. This is not a matter of linguistic snobbery. It is one of thoughtfulness, clarity of expression, and social responsibility. Speaking clearly and to the point requires effort and concentration, but is that too high a cost when we remember that our speech reflects the image of our Creator and Redeemer?

Finally, we should note that the Scriptures focus on language as the object of future salvation. The curse on the builders of the Tower of Babel continues to be a reminder of the presence of sin in our world. Appropriately, the prophet Zephaniah, in describing the end-times, gives us a divine promise: "Then will I purify the lips of the peoples, that all of them may call on the name of the LORD and serve him shoulder to shoulder" (Zeph. 3:9). Also, it has often been noted that on the Day of Pentecost, when the Holy Spirit enabled the apostles to speak in other tongues so that everyone heard others speaking in his own language (Acts 2:1–21), God appears to indicate a reversal of the Babel incident. We need not infer that linguistic uniformity is a goal of redemption, but surely the ability to understand each other and thus to praise God in unanimity is very much part of his saving grace to us.

When John tells us about the sound of "a great multitude, like the roar of rushing waters and like loud peals of thunder," he is not describing the confusion and cacophony of mixed linguistic communities, but the united voice of the redeemed (Rev. 19:6–7):

> Hallelujah!
> For our Lord God Almighty reigns.
> Let us rejoice and be glad
> and give him glory!

3

THE SCIENTIFIC STUDY
OF LANGUAGE

FUNDAMENTAL PRINCIPLES

As in any academic discipline, so also in linguistics controversy rages about many issues. The problem seems especially bad in linguistics, partly because of the relative newness of this field, partly because of its essentially interdisci plinary character (as we will see below, linguists argue not only among themselves, but also with students of literature, psychology, philosophy, etc.). For well over half a century, however, a set of principles has guided and given coherence to the mainstream of linguistic scholars. True, not every specialist would formulate these principles in the same way, and some respectable authorities may even wish to dissent with "the establishment" at a fundamental level. Still, we would do well to familiarize ourselves with those tenets that most clearly distinguish *modern* linguistics from previous stages in the study of language.

Synchronic Description

The label *synchronic description* covers two distinct concerns. (1) The term *description* contrasts with *prescription*: modern linguists see their task as one of discovery, analysis, and

41

explanation of how people actually use language. It is important to note that we are dealing here with a scholar's professional goal, not with what he or she may think is valuable in a more general setting. Just because linguists do not think they should make, say, economic pronouncements as part of their profession, we should not deduce that they believe economics is bad. Similarly, individual linguists may have very strong views about certain conventions in the English language. They may insist that their children say "Yes" rather than "Yeah"; they will readily correct a student who has used the word *imply* in a term paper where *infer* was the appropriate word. While they may therefore *prescribe* language use in certain situations, they would argue that as linguists they have a different job.

To be sure, some prominent linguists, particularly in the early decades of the discipline, did not always make this distinction clear. One popular work in the 1950s, for example, seemed to argue that no one in any situation ought to prescribe language use. Ironically, the author made the point in the title of the book by issuing a rather dramatic prescription himself: *Leave Your Language Alone!*[1] And one must further acknowledge that most linguists take a rather dim view of the traditional dos and don'ts taught in the schools, though the primary reason is that many of the rules are quite arbitrary and contradict the very genius of English.[2] But we cannot allow overstatements to obscure the basic issues, and our fundamental concern here is that the scientific study of language—whatever else we may or may not decide to do with language—should consist of careful description.

---

[1] Robert A. Hall, Jr., *Leave Your Language Alone!* (Ithaca, N.Y.: Linguistica, 1950). The second edition was wisely retitled *Linguistics and Your Language* (New York: Doubleday, 1960).

[2] For example, in his famous book, *Language: An Introduction to the Study of Speech* (New York: Harcourt, Brace & World, 1949, orig. 1921), pp. 156–63, Edward Sapir acknowledged that such a form as *Whom did you see?* could be viewed as "correct" on the analogy of I:me = he:him = who:whom. On the other hand, he gave four reasons why "there is something false about its correctness," in particular, the English rule that inflected objects must come *after* the verb. In other words, the popular tendency to say *Who did you see?* conforms to the bent of English grammar (though possibly not to that of Latin).

(2) The other term in our label is *synchronic* (= pertaining to one well-defined chronological period), which contrasts with *diachronic* (= developmental or historical). Perhaps no principle identifies more clearly the distinctive character of linguistics in its modern dress. Prior to this century, one could have found many scholars who indeed were interested in scientific description (rather than in telling people how to speak). But these scholars harnessed most of their energies for historical purposes. How do languages develop and change? What is the historical connection between related languages? How did languages originate? These were the all-consuming questions occupying linguists from the end of the eighteenth to the beginning of the twentieth century. And at least one prominent writer at the time could not "conceive how anyone can reflect with any advantage on a language without tracing to some extent the way in which it has historically developed."[3]

Around the turn of the century, however, a Swiss linguist by the name of Ferdinand de Saussure began to suggest to his students that such an approach was misguided. Saussure himself had done significant work in comparative Indo-European grammar, and he was certainly not about to propose that historical investigations be abandoned altogether. What he did object to was the implicit notion that a language can be adequately described by analyzing its development. Speakers are not normally conscious of the way their language *has come to be*; therefore, earlier stages of that language seldom play a role in their speech.

This principle is most clearly illustrated by the vocabulary, which changes more quickly than other linguistic elements. The English word *glamour*, for example, happens to be related to *grammar*.[4] Most speakers are completely unaware of

---

[3]Hermann Paul, *Principles of the History of Language* (London: Sonnenschein, 1890), p. xlvii, quoted by Roy Harris, *Reading Saussure: A Critical Commentary on the* Cours de linguistique générale (La Salle, Ill.: Open Court, 1987), p. 88. Harris, incidentally, offers a somewhat different interpretation of what the term *diachronic* implies. My comments, though in need of some nuancing, reflect a fairly standard approach that is adequate for our purposes.

[4]As early as the fifteenth century, the term *gramarye* (derived from *grammar*, "learning") was used of occult learning in particular, that is, magic. In the early

that connection, and so the connection is quite irrelevant to their use of either term. A linguist who wishes to describe how these terms function in a community of English speakers should therefore, according to Saussurean principles, ignore this interesting historical fact and describe the terms quite independently of one another. To use one of Saussure's best-known analogies, the chess game: the *position* of the pieces after ten moves will be *described* in exactly the same terms by an observer who comes in at that point as it would be by one who has watched the previous moves. Similarly, the main goal of the linguist is to describe how a language works at a specific stage or state (*synchrony*), not how it has evolved from one state to another (*diachrony*).[5]

Language as a Structured System[6]

Continuing the chess analogy, we can illustrate another fundamental Saussurean principle. A mere annotation of where

---

eighteenth century, Scottish altered *grammar* to *glamour* and used it in a further developed sense (that of *gramarye*), "magic spell." The word *glamour* then passed into more general English use, meaning "magic beauty" by the nineteenth century, then further it developed the meaning of "fascinating attraction."

[5]Saussure's class lectures were posthumously published by two of his students in 1916 and later rendered into English under the title, *Course in General Linguistics* (New York: Philosophical Library, 1959, repr. McGraw-Hill, 1966); see especially pp. 88–89. Much controversy surrounds both the text and the interpretation of this seminal work. The most reliable and complete edition is by R. Engler, *Edition critique du "Cours de linguistique générale" de F. de Saussure* (Wiesbaden: Harrassowitz, 1967). Note also Tullio de Mauro's edition (Paris: Payot, 1972). For a recent, and usually negative, interpretation, see Harris, *Reading Saussure*.

[6]The term *structuralism* has been appropriated by various disciplines, sometimes without sufficient rigor. It can be argued, for example, that the use of Saussurean ideas even by the renowned anthropologist C. Lévi-Strauss and the literary scholar R. Barthes depends on a fuzzy use of those ideas, mediated by the controversial linguist L. Hjelmslev. See the important criticisms by Martin Krampen, "Ferdinand de Saussure and the Development of Semiology," in *Classics of Semiotics*, ed. M. Krampen et al. (New York and London: Plenum, 1987), pp. 59–88, especially pp. 78–83. The further extension of similar terminology in biblical studies by proponents of "structural exegesis" (a misnomer in my opinion) has very little to do with linguistics.

each chess piece is located does not really explain the state of a particular game. On the contrary, there is a dynamic relationship among the pieces that reveals the true "meaning" of the game. Similarly, we do not do justice to language if we treat it atomistically, analyzing its individual components without reference to their place in the linguistic system.

The value of this observation was first demonstrated in connection with the sound system. Any individual learning a foreign language will quickly identify certain sounds that are present in his or her native language and notice other sounds that may prove difficult to master. Native English speakers, for example, will sense that they are already familiar with most Spanish consonants, such as the sounds represented by the letters *f, m,* and *s.* They may notice, to be sure, that some of these familiar consonants (e.g., *k, p, t*) are pronounced a little differently, though not enough to create problems of communication. Only a couple of sounds, such as the distinctive pronunciation of the *r,* appear to lie outside the sound system of English.

In fact, these impressions are based purely on the *physical* qualities of *individual* sounds, without regard for their connections with one another. A structural approach, on the other hand, assesses the significance of a sound by the role it plays within the system. For example, the fact that the letter *p* is pronounced in Spanish without the accompanying expulsion of breath (*aspiration*) characteristic of English has little linguistic significance.[7] English and Spanish possess the same trio of bilabial sounds (that is, articulated with both lips): the voiceless *p,* the voiced *b,* and the nasal *m.* Because that relationship is shared by both languages, we may say that the *p* "is the same" in both languages, that is, it plays basically the same role, has the same value.

In contrast, the letter *s* represents a sound that has the same physical characteristics in English as it does in Spanish, yet

---

[7]Indeed, English speakers pronounce the *p* just as Spanish speakers do in certain contexts, such as in the word *speaker* (the sound represented by the preceding letter *s* prevents aspiration; for an interesting experiment, hold your hand in front of your mouth as you alternately say the words *pin* and *spin*).

it has a different linguistic significance in each. The reason is simply that in English this voiceless sound (so-called because the vocal cords do not vibrate during its pronunciation) is paired with the voiced z, and such a distinction is nonexistent in Spanish.[8] Since therefore certain contrasts available in one language may not be available in another, linguists place emphasis on the concept of *opposition* as a key to the understanding of speech. This structural approach to phonology suggests that although sounds can be defined in positive terms (by the physical properties of voicing, place of articulation, etc.), their linguistic value is best defined negatively, that is, by their contrast to or difference from other sounds.[9]

Other elements of language, such as vocabulary, can be treated along similar lines. It is true, of course, that words are usually defined positively, suggesting a direct connection with their respective meanings. This possibility is especially clear with proper names: we can most easily "define" the word *Erasmus* by stating certain facts associated with the individual we refer to by that name. Other terms, however, seem to acquire their meaning by the way in which they are distinguished from other terms. Suppose that a teacher grades students by using three terms: *poor, average, good*. The area of meaning covered by *good* in this system is considerably larger than it would be if the teacher used five terms: *poor, average, good, excellent, exceptional*. More to the point, the word *good* means something quite different in each of these systems; that

---

[8]The letter z is not distinguished at all from the s in most Spanish-speaking countries. (In Castillian Spanish, spoken throughout most of Spain, z represents the sound of English *th* in *think*.)

[9]This kind of formulation relies heavily on the so-called Prague school of phonology. I am indebted to Emilio Alarcos Llorach, *Fonología española*, 4th ed. (BRE 3:1; Madrid: Gredos, 1968), especially p. 46. For a clear description of the American structural approach, see John Lyons, *Language and Linguistics: An Introduction* (Cambridge: Cambridge University Press, 1981), chap. 3. For the more recent generative perspective, now dominant, see the survey by Hans Basbøll, "Phonological Theory," *LTCS* 1:192–215, and the textbook by Roger Lass, *Phonology: An Introduction to Basic Concepts* (CTL; Cambridge: Cambridge University Press, 1984).

is, the meaning of the word seems determined by the presence or absence of related terms.

In short, the structural approach recognizes that linguistic facts are best studied, not as individual entities without relation to other facts, but as parts of a larger system. Moreover, it emphasizes that the significance of those facts is a function of their opposition or contrast to one another.

Language and Speech

A close examination of sound systems uncovers another interesting detail. The letter *l* in English represents two quite different sounds, depending on whether it is found at the beginning or the end of a syllable: contrast *leap* and *peal*. Because the difference in pronunciation is completely determined by the position of the sound, that difference cannot be used to distinguish words (as though the word *leap* could be pronounced in two different ways, each with a different meaning). As a result, most English speakers are not generally aware of this sound distinction, though in some other language the two sounds might be perceived as completely different.

For that matter, we should note that the "ell" sound is pronounced in a wide variety of ways: with sufficiently precise equipment, we could show that each individual (whether because of geographical "accent," physical differences in the organs of articulation, etc.) pronounces this sound in a slightly different way. Remarkably, speakers of English manage to make sense out of this phonetic mayhem and, quite unconsciously, abstract but one sound that is linguistically significant.[10]

This curious fact illustrates several features of language, but I mention it here primarily to emphasize the distinction

---

[10]Linguists use the term *phoneme* to describe such a significant sound; further, they enclose it within slashes to distinguish it from nonphonemic sounds, which are enclosed in square brackets. We would then say that the English letter *l* represents the phoneme / l /, and that this phoneme is "realized" (i.e., actually pronounced) in a variety of ways, primarily as the "clear" [l] and the "dark" or "velarized" [l].

between *langue* ("language" = a system that has the potential to become speech) and *parole* ("speech" = actual utterances). Saussure used those two French words to formulate a very important concept. According to Saussure, language [*langue*] "is a storehouse filled by the members of a given community through their active use of speaking"; it is "a grammatical system" with *potential* existence in individual brains. Moreover, "language is not complete in any speaker; it exists perfectly only within a collectivity."[11]

This distinction between *language* and *speech* is generally recognized as crucial, though linguists are not fully agreed as to which of the two is the proper object of linguistic study. Saussure himself argued for the former: he believed that the potential, but stable, system that is part of every speaker's consciousness is the appropriate field of investigation. During the past two or three decades, however, linguists have paid increasing attention to the striking amount of *variation* that characterizes actual speech. Such subjects as geographical differences, "social registers," bilingualism, and the broad category of *style* have become major fields of research. At the risk of oversimplification, we could say that most of the issues popularly associated with "grammar," insofar as they involve matters that leave little room for choice, belong in the category of language rather than speech. On the other hand, "what grammar leaves out"[12] is the area of style, where considerable variety exists among individuals, social groups, and geographical areas.

Other Principles

In addition to the matters already mentioned, most

---

[11]Saussure, *Course*, pp. 13–14. (Some theoreticians would regard *langue* as an abstract system, since it is possible to describe speakers as abstracting what is linguistically significant out of the specific and concrete instances of speaking. Saussure himself, however, regarded *langue* as concrete [ibid., p. 15].) Motivated by somewhat different concerns, the contemporary linguist Noam Chomsky, followed by many, has used the terms *competence* and *performance* in a way that corresponds, if only roughly, to the Saussurean distinction between *langue* and *parole*.

[12]G. W. Turner, *Stylistics* (Harmondsworth: Penguin, 1973), p. 19.

linguists work with certain assumptions that may be regarded as relatively obvious (though the word *relatively* has been known to cover a multitude of sins). For example, even a cursory acquaintance with modern linguistics reveals that its practitioners give primary, though not exclusive, attention to the spoken language. This approach reflects a "common sense" understanding that writing is a derivative form of language. To be sure, it would be difficult to prove conclusively that human beings spoke before they ever wrote (though the opposite viewpoint would seem to contradict what little information we have on this topic). It is enough to remind ourselves, however, that while there exist many societies that possess no written literature, all known linguistic communities consist of people who speak (unless physiologically impaired). More to the point, perhaps, is the fact that even in a modern society, where the written word has become exceedingly important, children learn to speak—indeed, they master the basic structure of their language—several years before they learn to read or write.

One should not deduce that linguists consider written literature unimportant. Here again we should note a distinction between what is and what is not the specific professional focus of the researcher. An individual linguist may indeed be a passionate lover of literature—he or she may even regard it as a more significant cultural symbol than the spoken form of language. The linguist recognizes, however, that written works by themselves tell us only how a small sample of a society uses language in a restricted number of activities. Literature, in other words, provides a truncated and thus inadequate base for determining how language actually works in a society.

Some readers may wonder how the linguist's concern for the "priority" of the spoken form affects our approach to Scripture, which by definition is *written*. Note, however, that as far as any philosophical aversion to writing is concerned, such an aversion goes back at least as far as Plato[13] and therefore

---

[13]See above, chap. 2, pp. 36–37. Cf. Paul Ricoeur, *Interpretation Theory: Discourse and the Surplus of Meaning* (Fort Worth: Texas Christian University Press, 1976), chap. 2, especially pp. 38–40. Ricoeur, who incidentally is not altogether a stranger to linguistic science, offers here an interesting, and in many

could not have originated from recent developments in linguistics. Although one could probably find linguists on both sides of this philosophical question, the *methodological* issue at hand is of quite a different character, since it seeks merely to define the proper object of scientific inquiry, not the relative merits or validity of these two forms of language. Moreover, we should keep in mind that, while we have no access to the spoken form of many ancient languages (including of course Old Testament Hebrew and New Testament Greek), *general* linguistics seeks to formulate principles and rules that are characteristic of human language as such, not necessarily those that belong exclusively to specific languages. Therefore, many of the results arising from modern linguistic research are applicable even to communities in the past for which a spoken form is not extant.

This brings us to our last introductory concept, namely, that modern linguists are interested in all languages alike. Prior to the twentieth century, the influence of classical culture led students to pay disproportionate attention to Greek and Latin, and it was often assumed that the particular structure of these languages ("synthetic" or "inflecting") evinced a higher order of thought. In contrast, so-called "analytical" languages (such as English, in which nominal case endings and verbal conjugations play a less important role) were thought inferior—to say nothing of "agglutinative" languages like Turkish. This preju-

_____

(though not all) respects powerful, philosophical defense of writing. Less restrained, but still worthy of note, is Etienne Gilson, *Linguistics and Philosophy: An Essay on the Philosophical Constants of Language* (Notre Dame, Ind.: University of Notre Dame Press, 1988): "Every writer concerned with the quality of his work and aware of its nature knows that the written thought is not a simple record of the spoken thought but is another thought, conceived with a view to writing and obedient to its own laws" (p. 131); "writing is not just the husk of the spoken word, . . . for it . . . does with and for language . . . many things of which the spoken word is incapable" (p. 132); "born of the spoken language from which it remains inseparable, the written language confers upon it, nevertheless, a peculiar status, as of an empire within an empire, a permanent refuge of the works of the most true and most beautiful intelligence. It is a holy and quasi-divine domain, in the strict sense of the term, for in the written the spoken endures, and in the spoken the intellect lives, a witness in man of a power of creation superior to man" (p. 146).

dice was sometimes taken to curious extremes: "One celebrated American writer on culture and language delivered himself of the dictum that, estimable as the speakers of agglutinative languages might be, it was nevertheless a crime for an inflecting woman to marry an agglutinative man."[14]

The careful study of American Indian languages and other "primitive" cultures early in this century, however, had a powerful impact on this point of view. And well it should. Anyone who had previously thought that grammatical complexity was a sign of advanced culture could not help but be shocked. If the inflections of the classical languages represented sophisticated logic (each adjective, for example, must be marked for case, number, and gender), what was one to do with the Bantu languages, which mark nouns according to various classes on the basis of such contrasts as person/nonperson and countable/uncountable? And if the many conjugations of the Greek verb appeared daunting, the Basque verb could only be described as "impossible"![15]

These facts do not of course diminish the great achievements of classical culture, nor do they minimize the beauty of its literature. That greatness and beauty, however, do not inhere in the grammatical structure of Greek and Latin; rather, they are the result of great minds using those languages to their full potential. Moreover, the question that concerns us here is not whether certain languages may be more esthetically pleasing than others. Even the most committed linguist, no doubt, has personal preferences about that sort of thing. What really matters is the willingness to take seriously all the linguistic

---

[14]Sapir, *Language*, p. 124, n. 2. In modern dress: "Some of my best friends are agglutinative. . . ."

[15]*El imposible vencido* ("The Impossible Conquered") was in fact the title of a Spanish grammar of the Basque verb. See Otto Jespersen, *Language: Its Nature, Development, and Origin* (New York: Norton, 1964, orig. 1921), p. 427. Jespersen adds, "At Béarn they have the story that the good God, wishing to punish the devil for the temptation of Eve, sent him to the Pays Basque with the command that he should remain there till he had mastered the language. At the end of seven years God relented, finding the punishment too severe, and called the devil to him. The devil had no sooner crossed the bridge of Castelondo than he found he had forgotten all that he had so hardly learned."

evidence, wherever it may come from, and to use it responsibly in the formulation of theories and principles.

THE INTERDISCIPLINARY OUTLOOK

Even a shallow exposure to linguistics quickly reveals that the study of language cannot be confined to the approaches used by one or two academic disciplines. Consciously or not, students of language have always had to use an interdisciplinary technique. During the past few decades, however, this feature has become so prominent that one may wonder whether it is any longer possible to think of linguistics as a specific discipline. We can best survey the landscape by using the conventional threefold division of higher education: humanities, natural sciences, and social sciences.

The Humanities

For many of us, the study of language is primarily the province of the humanities. After all, our elementary and secondary education includes this field under the general rubric of *language arts*. And indeed, modern universities often explore the subject matter of linguistics within the curriculum of English studies and foreign languages (including classics). Moreover, and obviously, there is a close interface between the fields of literature and language, especially in the related areas of stylistics and rhetorical criticism. It should be pointed out, however, that in some English and foreign language departments the study of language is not well integrated with *modern* linguistics; indeed, the latter may be ignored altogether.

Insofar as *history* is perceived as a humanistic field (usually it is brought together with the social sciences), one can also see a close relationship between it and language study. As we will notice in the next chapter, linguistics must deal with the reality of language development even if it does not consider such a development its primary concern. The tools honed by the historical method, as well as the evidence uncovered by historical investigation, provide an essential service to linguists, some of whom fully integrate the two disciplines in their own careers.

Then there is *philosophy*. The earliest serious discussions of language known to us were carried on by ancient Greek philosophers. While their primary concerns—both then and in later centuries—were rather broad and speculative in character, they managed to make important (empirical) observations that continue to hold the interest of language students. Moreover, the technical field of logic is closely bound to the character of language. At the beginning of this century, however, philosophical thought experienced something of a revolution that came to be known as "the linguistic turn."[16] Tired of the abstract quality of the so-called idealist tradition, such brilliant British thinkers as G. E. Moore and Bertrand Russell decided that the real task of philosophy was to clarify our concepts and therefore our language. The Austrian Ludwig Wittgenstein and other prominent philosophers took up this theme and generated a new subdiscipline known as Analytic Philosophy. (The question of "God-talk," which we have broached in chapter 2, often emerges in this context and so overlaps with the concerns of *religious studies*.)

Although working independently of twentieth-century linguistic science, these philosophers developed principles and methods that were very similar indeed to what linguists were doing.[17] The isolation between linguists and philosophers has gradually given way to cooperation, and it is no longer unusual to find philosophers fully abreast of developments in linguistics or linguists who capably try their hand at philosophical

---

[16]Cf. Richard Rorty, ed., *The Linguistic Turn: Recent Essays in Philosophical Method* (Chicago: University of Chicago Press, 1967). It is important to distinguish "philosophy of language," which indicates one of the subject matters of philosophy, from "linguistic (or analytical) philosophy," which refers to a particular method of doing philosophy.

[17]The prominent linguist Stephen Ullmann, in *The Principles of Semantics*, 2d ed. (New York: Philosophical Library, 1957), p. 137, expressed surprise to find out that Wittgenstein's ideas paralleled developments in linguistics. Cf. also James Barr, *Biblical Words for Time*, 2d ed. (SBT 1/33; London: SCM, 1969), p. 197.

investigation.[18] Nevertheless, one must be careful not to blur some important distinctions between the two disciplines. In particular, it is unhelpful and misleading to assume that all modern linguists share the *philosophical* commitments of analytical philosophers (except in the very general sense that a valid philosophy of language must build on an accurate understanding of human language).

In addition to the disciplines already mentioned, it may not be far-fetched to recognize some links between language study and the fine arts. It isn't just a matter of the commonplace that "artists are trying to communicate something." Both painting and music, along with language, may be said to be part of the broader field of *semiotics* (the science of signs): "Sounds in music work as elements of a system and acquire a value according to specific criteria of pertinence: a primitive who makes timbre pertinent instead of pitch perceives as the same melody what a European feels as two different melodies played on two different instruments."[19] But analogies of this type should not be pressed. And while phoneticians may profitably use musical notations to describe "suprasegmental" features of speech (tempo, pitch, etc.), we need not fear the development of a new hybrid known as "musicolinguists."

The Natural Sciences

At the other end of the academic spectrum stand the so-called hard sciences. Toward the end of the nineteenth century, comparative philologists who came to be known as Neogram-

---

[18]Cf. Colin Lyas, ed., *Philosophy and Linguistics* (New York: Macmillan, 1971). For the most recent developments, see Alice ter Meulen, "Linguistics and the Philosophy of Language," *LTCS* 1:430–46.

[19]Umberto Eco, "The Influence of Roman Jakobson on the Development of Semiotics," in *Classics of Semiotics* (ed. Krampen et al.), pp. 109–27, quotation from p. 120. Leonard Bernstein, in one of his TV series, was daring enough to use the terminology and principles of transformational grammar to explain various features of music. Although a few of his analogies were thought-provoking, one must not think that he effected an *integration* of the two disciplines. See *The Unanswered Question: Six Talks at Harvard (The Charles Eliot Norton Lectures)* (Cambridge, Mass.: Harvard University Press, 1976).

marians were able to demonstrate the presence of "laws" (that is, clear regularities) in sound changes. As a result, they claimed, their discipline had become a science. Is there a genuine integration between the sciences and linguistics?

The most obvious point of contact is in the field of *acoustics*. For a phonetician to be able to understand and describe speech sounds, he or she must have a strong grounding in the physics of sound. To be precise, however, phonetics is not linguistics, but rather an ancillary discipline.

Another area of interaction is that of *biology*. Both zoologists and paleontologists contribute to various aspects of linguistics, such as the debated question of language origin and the problems associated with language development in children. Of particular value is the work of researchers in the field of neurology, which is able to examine the control of the human brain over speech processes (this field is closely related to that of *psycholinguistics*; see below).[20]

The most fruitful field is *mathematics* broadly considered. Some linguists have attempted to describe language through algebraic concepts. More productive still has been the application of statistics to language study. We can predict, for example, that the fifteen most common words in any language will make up about 25 percent of the total words used in a (sufficiently long) sample text; more than half of the total words in the text will consist of the one hundred most frequently used words. It has also been demonstrated that an inverse relation ship exists between the length of a word and its frequency of use. Statistics such as these are not mere curiosities: they shed light on the way language is structured and functions.[21]

Of special importance is the contribution of communica-

[20]Cf. David Caplan, "The Biological Basis for Language," *LTCS* 3:237–55; Sheila E. Blumstein, "Neurolinguistics: An Overview of Language-Brain Relations in Aphasia," ibid., pp. 210–36.

[21]The statistical study of language owes much to the writings of G. K. Zipf and G. U. Yule. For a very rigorous study, which includes a discussion of stylostatistics, see Gustav Herdan, *The Advanced Theory of Language as Choice and Chance* (Kommunikation und Kybernetik in Einzeldarstellungen 4; New York: Springer-Verlag, 1966).

tion engineering, in particular information theory.[22] The mathematical analysis of what is involved in the transmission of information has led to major discoveries. For example, we have become aware of the value and need for *redundancy* in language: if language were perfectly efficient, then even the slightest *noise* (a technical term referring to any type of distortion) would hamper communication. It has also become clear that *uncertainty* is a requirement for conveying information. If a unit of language is completely certain or predictable (e.g., *to* in *I want to eat* —the speaker has no choice but to use this particle if he wants to speak with acceptable grammar), it communicates no information; on the other hand, the greater the degree of choice or uncertainty, the greater the measure of information conveyed.[23]

Finally, we must note the growing significance of computer science, with its own "programming languages," its progress in machine translation, its use for information retrieval, and its promise of artificial intelligence. Yet for all the real contributions of the sciences, it would be difficult to maintain that these disciplines are the most appropriate context for the study of language. Language is foremost a social activity. Accordingly, linguistics is usually viewed as belonging to the behavioral sciences.

The Social Sciences

There is much to be said for the view that linguistics is primarily an *anthropological* field. Indeed, most of the progress

---

[22]For a wide-ranging, lively, and provocative treatment, see Jeremy Campbell, *Grammatical Man: Information, Entropy, Language, and Life* (New York: Simon and Schuster, 1982). One need not follow Campbell's fertile imagination in every respect to appreciate the validity of many of the connections he draws in his book. Cf. especially chap. 5 on redundancy. For a more technical treatment, see Herdan, *Advanced Theory*, §§ 15–17.

[23]To be pedantically precise: "The amount of information in any signal is the logarithm to the base two of the reciprocal of the probability of that signal. That is: $I = \text{Log}_2\ 1/p$." See H. A. Gleason, Jr., *An Introduction to Descriptive Linguistics*, rev. ed. (New York: Holt, Rinehart and Winston, 1961), p. 377, for an explanation!

made in the modern study of language in North America was accomplished by anthropologists who worked with various American Indian groups. This important field continues to contribute essential information about the relationship between cultural patterns and language expression.[24]

Closely related to these concerns are those of *sociology*. At this point we certainly meet a complete integration between two fields of study, so that we can accurately refer to the new discipline of *sociolinguistics*.[25] Much of the growth in this field is directly related to the view that the proper object of linguistics is not *langue*, as Saussure suggested, but rather *parole*, that is, the actual utterances of people in specific contexts. Questions of social stratification, politics, sexism, verbal art, humor, bilingualism, style, and many more are seen to be essential for a proper understanding of language. This new approach has also generated interest in discourse analysis (see chap. 6).

Finally, there are some who would argue that the study of language is essentially *psycholinguistics*. One of the most influential linguists in America is Noam Chomsky, who, beginning in the 1950s, developed a view of language that challenged the behaviorism of B. F. Skinner. Impressed by the ability of children to create new sentences that they had never heard before, he argued that human beings have an innate capacity to learn and use language. In connection with this insight he developed a new method of language description, closely tied to psychological investigation, which came to be known as *transformational* (or *generative*) grammar.[26]

---

[24]For some interesting illustrations, see Robbins Burling, *Man's Many Voices: Language in Its Cultural Context* (New York: Holt, Rinehart and Winston, 1970), especially chaps. 2–5.

[25]See the survey by Beatriz R. Lavandera, "The Study of Language in Its Socio-Cultural Context," *LTCS* 4:1–13, and the rest of the chapters in the same volume. The more narrowly focused field of *ethnolinguistics* could be viewed as a subdivision of either sociology or anthropology.

[26]Because transformational linguists depend heavily on native speakers (including themselves) to determine whether utterances are grammatical, this approach has not been vigorously applied to the study of ancient languages. For an attempt to do so, cf. Daryl Dean Schmidt, *Hellenistic Greek Grammar and*

Psycholinguists, however, are primarily interested in such questions as the neurological role of the brain in the production of speech, the development of speech in children, the analogies between human speech and animal communication, the effects of bilingualism, the more general relationships between thought and language, and so on.[27] It is obvious that some of the challenges faced by anthropologists and sociologists (e.g., what effect culture has on language and vice-versa) cannot be adequately met without the help of psycholinguistics.

Even this important field, however, cannot claim absolute rights over the study of language. Indeed, whether we view linguistics as belonging primarily to the behavioral sciences or to the humanities, this discipline must be viewed as both an independent field of study and one that is inherently amenable to interdisciplinary research.

Noam Chomsky: Nominalizing Transformations (SBLDS 62; Chico, Calif.: Scholars Press, 1981).

[27]See Michael K. Tanenhaus, "Psycholinguistics: An Overview," *LTCS* 3:1–37, and the rest of the chapters in the same volume.

4
THE HISTORICAL DIMENSION

Although modern linguistics, as we have seen, places less emphasis on the diachronic (or historical) approach than on the synchronic, one must not conclude that historical considerations are unimportant. In particular, students of ancient literature sometimes face problems that require historical research. One obvious example is the occurrence of words referring to cultural artifacts that no longer exist. The attempt to discover information about an earlier culture is, to be sure, an *extra*-linguistic task not to be confused with the analysis of a linguistic system, but it would be artificial to draw a sharp dichotomy between language and culture.

Besides, there are other, more subtle, problems. If we are studying the Lord's Prayer, we will need to deal with the rare word *epiousios*, usually translated "daily" (Matt. 6:11; Luke 11:3). Because the word does not occur elsewhere in the New Testament, or for that matter in other Greek literature (except for later Christian writers quoting the Gospels), scholars need to consider the possible derivation of the word: Does it mean "necessary for existence" (*epi* + *ousia*), or "for the current day" (*epi tēn ousan hēmeran*), or "for the following day" (*hē epiousa hēmera*)? In order to come up with these and other options, one has to consider the etymology of the word—a diachronic exercise. This kind of problem, incidentally, while very unusual in the Greek New Testament, is faced with some frequency by Old Testament scholars.

We may, and should, insist that a language be described according to the way it is used at a particular chronological stage (synchronic description). But a broad knowledge of the prehistory, as well as the historical development, of the language can help the student handle certain linguistic difficulties.[1]

LANGUAGE FAMILIES

Among historical questions, few are more challenging than those addressed by the comparative method. This method was in effect born toward the end of the eighteenth century, when Sir William Jones, having carefully studied Sanskrit, the ancient language of India, discovered similarities between it and the classic European languages that could hardly be explained as accidental. The likelihood that Greek, Latin, and Sanskrit had all developed from one common language sparked the interest of scholars, and a tremendous amount of intellectual energy during the nineteenth century was expended on refining comparative techniques.

We can demonstrate, for example, that there is such a thing as a *Romance* family of languages—comprising French, Italian, Portuguese, Rumanian, Spanish, etc.—that has descended from Latin. Similarly, such languages as Danish, Dutch, English, German, Gothic (an ancient language no longer spoken), Norwegian, and Swedish are closely related and belong to the *Germanic* family, even though in this case the parent language (comparable to Latin for the Romance tongues) has not survived. Linguists refer to this parent language as Proto-Germanic and attempt to reconstruct it on the basis of the evidence provided by the languages that have survived.

Moreover, the Romance and Germanic families can be

---

[1]Cf. the treatment of Greek phonology in chap. 5. For a wide-ranging survey, including the comparative method, structuralist and transformationalist models, and issues of language contact, see Theodora Bynon, *Historical Linguistics* (CTL; Cambridge: Cambridge University Press, 1977).

shown to have developed from a common "proto"-language. Thus we could speak of French and English as "cousins," for example. Indeed, English speakers can recognize many similarities between their language and French. Some of these similarities, of course, are the result of cultural contact: in earlier centuries English *borrowed* heavily from French (e.g., *closet, depart, faith, joy, president, prestige*),[2] while recently French has become influenced by English (e.g., *drugstore, sexy, weekend*). But other resemblances, such as the basic vocabulary of numbers (English *one, two, three*; French *un, deux, trois*), can only be explained on the assumption of a common descent.

Further research shows that the Romance and Germanic languages, in addition, are closely related to other families, such as *Celtic* (e.g., the Gaelic spoken in Scotland), *Balto-Slavic* (Russian, Polish, etc.), *Indo-Iranian* (Sanskrit, Hindi, Persian, etc.), and others. We can therefore subsume all of these important languages under one large category known as *Indo-European*, and some scholars devote their research to determine what Proto-Indo-European must have looked like. The evidence that certain words must indeed go back to a time before the subfamilies developed is of interest not only to linguists, but also to students of prehistorical culture. Archaeological evidence thus goes hand in hand with reconstructed linguistic data.[3] For our purposes, we need only keep in mind that Greek belongs to this Indo-European family.

Hebrew and Aramaic, on the other hand, belong to the *Semitic* family of languages.[4] This family is often subdivided

---

[2]Among many fine histories of English, note Albert C. Baugh and Thomas Cable, *A History of the English Language*, 3d ed. (Englewood Cliffs, N.J.: Prentice Hall, 1978).

[3]For a recent hypothesis, see A. Colin Renfrew, *Archaeology and Language: The Puzzle of Indo-European Origins* (Cambridge: Cambridge University Press, 1988). Cf. also T. V. Gamkrelidze and V. V. Ivanov, "The Early History of Indo-European Languages," *Scientific American* 262 no. 3 (March 1990): 110–16.

[4]More precisely, we should expand the family to include Egyptian and related languages. The older term used to describe this broader family, *Hamito-Semitic*, has given way to *Afro-Asiatic*; cf. Carleton T. Hodge, "Afroasiatic: An Overview," in Thomas A. Sebeok, ed., *Current Trends in Linguistics*, vol. 6 (The Hague and Paris: Mouton, 1970), pp. 237–54. Furthermore, some scholars

into (1) an eastern branch, known as Akkadian, consisting of Babylonian and Assyrian dialects; (2) a southern branch, which includes Arabic, Ethiopic, and South Arabian; and (3) a northwestern branch.[5] Our main interest is in this last branch, *Northwest Semitic*, which is usually further subdivided into two main groups, *Canaanite* (consisting of Phoenician, Moabite, Hebrew, etc.) and *Aramaic* (various forms, including Jewish Palestinian Aramaic, Syriac, Mandean, etc.).

This kind of information can be very useful in our appreciation of the languages involved. For example, many students of the Bible tend to assume that Aramaic, as spoken by Jews in New Testament times, was a late and inferior (corrupt?) dialect of Hebrew. In fact, however, we may describe the relationship between Hebrew and Aramaic as analogous to that of "close cousins"—an even closer relationship than that between, say, English and German. (Aramaic, incidentally, had a long and, from a political point of view, more distinguished history than Hebrew. More on this question below.)

---

believe that behind the Indo-European and Afroasiatic families there lies an older common root. Even if this theory is true, most linguists doubt that we will ever have the evidence necessary to prove it. On the difficulties of defining Semitic characteristics, see the well-known article by E. Ullendorff, "What Is a Semitic Language?" *Orientalia* NS 27 (1958): 66–75, reprinted in *Is Biblical Hebrew a Language? Studies in Semitic Languages and Civilizations* (Wiesbaden: Harrassowitz, 1977), pp. 155–71.

[5]For a convenient handbook, see Sabatino Moscati et al., *An Introduction to the Comparative Grammar of Semitic Languages: Phonology and Morphology* (Porta linguarum orientalium, n.s. 6; Wiesbaden: Harrassowitz, 1964). Cf. also Edward Ullendorff, "Comparative Semitics," in *Current Trends* (ed. Sebeok) 6:261–73, and Peter T. Daniels' important translation and updating of Gotthelf Bergsträsser, *Introduction to the Semitic Languages* (Winona Lake, Ind.: Eisenbrauns, 1983; orig. 1928). The threefold division mentioned above, while convenient, oversimplifies the facts. Some linguists seem increasingly reluctant to develop neat arrangements of this sort. The discovery of Ugaritic and Eblite, in particular, has not only increased our knowledge but also created considerable debate. See, for example, the articles by I. M. Diakonoff and W. von Soden in *Studies on the Language of Ebla*, ed. Pelio Fronzaroli (Quaderni di semitistica 13; Florence: Università di Firenze, 1984). For a new proposal, building on the work of R. Hetzron (who argued that Arabic is not part of South Semitic but belongs with Canaanite and Aramaic), see Rainer M. Voigt, "The Classification of Central Semitic," *Journal of Semitic Studies* 32 (1987): 1–21, especially the diagram on p. 15.

The sound inventory of Hebrew, for example, was basically identical to that of Aramaic,[6] but different in some important respects from the inventory of other Semitic languages, such as Arabic (which preserved several additional consonants) and Akkadian (which lost a number of consonantal distinctions). Hebrew and Aramaic also shared a large number of vocabulary items; not a few of them were pronounced a little differently ("gold" = Heb. *zahab*, Aram. *dehab*), but as a rule the similarities were quite obvious. Some of the more significant differences include the structure of the verbal system and the way in which definiteness is indicated: Hebrew, in a manner roughly comparable to English and Greek, uses a definite article attached to the front of the noun, whereas Aramaic adds something like a suffix (usually the vowel -*a* is attached to the end of the noun).

What needs to be appreciated, in any case, is that Hebrew and Aramaic, along with the other Semitic languages, differ greatly from Greek and the other Indo-European languages. With regard to the sound system, Greek does not have a series of consonants, popularly described as "gutturals" and "emphatics," that are distinctive of Semitic. But even those consonants that are found both in Greek and in Hebrew/Aramaic cannot be simply identified: the respective sound *structures* are quite unlike each other, and so the sounds in question "behave" differently. The phonological differences are most obvious in the case of the vowels, which are used in Semitic primarily to alter the grammatical function of words.[7] That, incidentally, is the reason Hebrew speakers can easily read

---

[6]This comment, as well as others in the subsequent discussion, need qualification. The oldest inscriptions, for example, suggest that Aramaic, at that stage, preserved some "proto-Semitic" sounds not attested at all in Hebrew.

[7]Most Hebrew words consist of three consonants (the root), while the vowel patterns are in general the same for the different roots. The vast majority of verbs, for example, use a specific vowel pattern for the simple third masculine singular form (*katab*, "he wrote"; *'ahab*, "he loved," etc.). One thus would never find two different Hebrew verbs that had the same consonants but that could be distinguished merely by their use of different vowel patterns, something quite possible in Indo-European (cf. English *kill/call*, *bag/beg*, *arm/ram*).

a text that consists only of consonants (indeed, Hebrew and other Semitic languages were written for many centuries before a full system for indicating vowels was introduced).

The vocabulary of Greek is also vastly different from that of Hebrew. Rarely does one find a pair of corresponding words that have the same meaning in both languages and also sound somewhat alike. In some of these cases, the similarities are purely coincidental; in other instances, they reflect cultural contact rather than a genetic connection (e.g., Greek *sakkos*, "sack, coarse garment," corresponds to Hebrew *saq* because the early Greeks borrowed the word from the Phoenicians). The disparities between the two language families become even more significant when one examines the grammar. The Hebrew and Aramaic verbs are built on several different stems (each of which includes a prefixed and a suffixed conjugation),[8] while the Greek verbs follow a complicated system of moods and tenses/aspects. A Hebrew narrative is typically made up of simple sentences linked by the conjunction "and," but Greek relies on a variety of conjunctions as well as complex subordinate clauses (especially with the rich use of the participle).

Many other details could be listed to illustrate the systematic differences between Greek (as a representative of Indo-European) and Hebrew/Aramaic (as representatives of Semitic). On the other hand, one should avoid exaggerating these differences, as though they implied widely divergent worldviews that made communication impossible. One of the strengths of modern linguistics lies precisely in its universal focus. Without minimizing the peculiarities of each language, linguists seek to understand the nature of language *as such*. At

---

[8]For example, the simple stem *zkr* means "remember," while the so-called causative stem *hzkr* means "remind" (= cause to remember). Other basic verbal concepts, such as reflexive activity, the passive voice, repetitive action, and so on, are likewise indicated by using different stems. (See the full discussion of verbal stems in Waltke and O'Connor, *Biblical Hebrew Syntax*, chap. 21.) Moreover, the first person singular (simple stem) takes the form *'ezkor* in the prefixed or imperfect conjugation (used of nonperfective aspect and often translated with a future, "I will remember"), while in the suffixed or perfect conjugation the form is *zakarti* (often translated with a past tense, "I remembered"). See also below, chap. 6, pp. 111–18.

the most fundamental level, Greek, Hebrew, and Aramaic share all the features that constitute them, quite simply, as human languages.

We have not yet addressed, however, the practical question: What value does the comparative method have for the *interpretation* of texts (biblical or otherwise)? In all frankness, not much. When Jeremiah or Paul spoke and wrote, they did so without knowledge of "language families"—much less would they have been aware of the specific prehistorical connections that modern scholars have established. In other words, the biblical writings have to be understood in the context of what their respective authors knew and meant to say. For example, the evidence from Sanskrit makes clear that Greek, in an earlier form no longer extant, used eight grammatical cases. This piece of information is useful for certain technical questions, but it is misleading to say, as some grammar books do, that New Testament Greek has eight cases.[9] Thus the significance of, say, the genitive case in a particular New Testament passage has to be deduced from the use of the genitive in first-century Greek; it cannot be determined by reading into the first-century writers grammatical features that existed in prehistoric times.

I do not mean to suggest, however, that comparative linguistics has no place or relevance in biblical scholarship. On the contrary. For one thing, it can prove utterly fascinating. Students of Greek often feel frustrated when they come across irregularities that seem to have no rhyme or reason. Being able to account for these irregularities will not help them learn Greek better (English speakers understand their native language quite well even though they have little idea why the past tense of *break* is not *breaked*). Often, however, it is both exciting and encouraging to discover that there is an answer for something that seemed unexplainable—much as some people feel exhilarated when they find out how a complicated machine works and are thereby stimulated to learn more.

Of greater importance, however, is the fact that we do need people who know how to repair the machine when it

---

[9]Note the discussion in chap. 6, p. 103–4.

breaks! Not everybody is cut out for this sort of thing. Nor is it necessary for someone to know how to tune up an engine in order to go out for a drive. Similarly, a biblical interpreter can understand New Testament Greek quite well—indeed, he or she could be an expert exegete—without being able to explain why, for example, certain third-declension nouns are accented on the antepenult even though the ultima is long.[10] Behind the scenes, however, specialists are needed who can control the data and provide a coherent explanation.

In addition, there are times when we come across important texts that are fraught with obscurities, and a firm historical and comparative knowledge can provide possible answers. Because the Greek language is so richly attested, the evidence from Greek itself is almost always sufficient to clarify difficult texts in the New Testament and contemporary literature. The Hebrew Old Testament, however, contains a significant number of passages (especially in such poetic books as Job) that cannot be understood without some help from the cognate languages. Even in the case of Hebrew, the comparative approach cannot hold primacy, since contextual considerations are more relevant than what a cognate word or grammatical form may have meant in a distant language such as Arabic.[11] It would be foolhardy to deny, however, that some

---

[10]I mention this example because, when I came across the problem in my first year of Greek study, it well-nigh destroyed my confidence in the rationality of the Greek language! The answer is fairly simple, once we become acquainted with the history of early Greek dialects. That history makes clear that, at the stage when this phonological rule about accents was operative, the form was different: *poleos* (genitive case), that is, with a short ultima (and a long penult), which allows the accent to go back to the antepenult. *After* this rule ceased to operate in the living speech, however, the form in question in the Attic dialect went through a metathesis (or transposition) of vowel length, *poleos*. By this time, however, the accent was firmly in place and thus Attic (and the related Koine) ended up with a set of irregular forms.

[11]The abuse of this method has been carefully documented by James Barr, *Comparative Philology and the Text of the Old Testament* (Oxford: Clarendon Press, 1968). Comparative work is especially useful in deciphering languages newly discovered, such as Ugaritic a couple of generations ago.

facility in Comparative Semitics is very important to gain expertise in Old Testament exegesis.

LINGUISTIC DEVELOPMENT

Apart from the comparative method, historical concerns can also prove valuable when we restrict ourselves to individual languages in their *attested* forms. (Comparative philology is primarily interested in reconstructing the prehistorical—that is, unattested—forms.) Tracing the development of a language can focus on either external or internal history. External history refers to broad cultural questions: Who spoke Aramaic and where? How widespread was its use? What factors influenced its development? What kind of literature was produced with it? What impact did it have on civilization? Internal history, on the other hand, has to do with linguistic change as such: Did Greek lose or gain specific consonantal sounds in the course of its development? Was its syntax simplified or made more complex? To what extent did the meanings of words change? These two kinds of concerns cannot always be separated from one another, but keeping the distinction in mind helps clarify some of the issues involved.

Hebrew and Aramaic

Quite possibly, Abraham, whose relatives resided in an Aramean region north of Palestine, spoke a very ancient form of Aramaic at the time he entered Canaan.[12] It is reasonable to suppose that he and his descendants adopted the closely related language spoken by their Canaanite neighbors. In the course of time, this Canaanite language would have developed into

---

[12]For a recent and capable discussion of the history of the Arameans, see Wayne T. Pitard, *Ancient Damascus: A Historical Study of the Syrian City-State from Earliest Times until Its Fall to the Assyrians in 732 B.C.E.* (Winona Lake, Ind.: Eisenbrauns, 1987). His own conclusions regarding the data from Genesis are cautiously stated: "There is no reason why there could not have been some relation between the ancestors of Israel and ancestors of the Aramaean tribes who set up the states in Syria at the end of the second millennium" (p. 87).

distinct forms corresponding to tribal groupings. Accordingly, Canaanite as spoken by the Hebrews became a distinct language and would have been viewed as one of many dialects spoken in Palestine and surrounding areas. And although the prestige of Hebrew would have grown significantly with the development of the Davidic and Solomonic monarchies (10th–9th centuries B.C.), it does not appear to have had much influence outside the Israelite boundaries.

In contrast, Aramaic became an international language in the Ancient Near East. The biblical narrative itself reflects this situation in the well-known story of Sennacherib's invasion of Judah. When the Assyrian king sent his field commander to threaten the people in Jerusalem, the Hebrew officials requested, "Please speak to your servants in Aramaic, since we understand it. Don't speak to us in Hebrew in the hearing of the people on the wall" (2 Kings 18:26). Subsequently, after the destruction of Jerusalem by the Babylonians, the Hebrews taken captive to Babylon adopted Aramaic (including the so-called "square script," used even today to write Hebrew) as a common means of communication. Those who returned to Palestine preserved both Hebrew and Aramaic, though Aramaic seemed to gain increasingly popular acceptance, especially among the Jews who lived in Galilee.[13]

After the close of the New Testament era, the Jewish state was destroyed (A.D. 135). Many Jews remained in some areas of Palestine, such as Tiberias, and continued to use Aramaic, whereas Hebrew was restricted more and more to academic contexts and writing. A similar situation obtained among the Jews in Babylon and other eastern settings. Throughout the Middle Ages and the modern period, Hebrew was not a living, spoken language. At the end of the nineteenth century, however, the language experienced an astonishing revival, and upon the emergence of the modern state of Israel in 1948, Hebrew took its place as a vital, national tongue.

---

[13]See the thorough survey by Joseph A. Fitzmyer, *A Wandering Aramean: Collected Aramaic Essays* (SBLMS 25; Missoula, Mont.: Scholars Press, 1979), chap. 2.

The use of Aramaic continued to be much more wide-spread than that of Hebrew in late antiquity. Pockets of Aramaic-speaking communities in Palestine survived into modern times. So-called Eastern Aramaic had a particularly vibrant history, especially through a dialect known to modern scholars as Syriac (not to be confused with the language of the modern state of Syria, where Arabic is spoken). Christians in the environments of Antioch and in other population centers of the Near East, such as Edessa, but also as far as India, spoke this form of Aramaic and produced a very significant body of literature.[14]

Tracing the internal or linguistic changes of Hebrew and Aramaic is beset by certain complications. In the case of Aramaic, those changes are closely tied to dialectal variation. The Aramaic of the earliest inscriptions certainly shows some differences from that of the fifth-century B.C. Egyptian papyri (discovered in Elephantine), and this stage in turn must be distinguished from the later Aramaic documents discovered in Qumran. Unfortunately, however, there is no clear continuity between these various stages.

In the case of Hebrew, we do have a richer literary tradition extending for several centuries, but here too some obstacles stand in the way. In the first place, there is considerable debate concerning the date of some of the books of the Old Testament. Moreover, it appears that the text went through a linguistic updating; most likely, for example, the spelling may have been standardized toward the end of the biblical period, thus removing traces of earlier grammatical differences. Nevertheless, scholars would be in general agreement that some poetic portions of the Old Testament—notably the Song of Deborah in Judges 5—preserve archaic features going back beyond the first millennium B.C., while the Books of Chronicles represent the Hebrew spoken in postexilic Judah as late as the fourth century B.C.

---

[14]Survivors of this Christian tradition in northern Iraq and Iran refer to themselves as Assyrians. Another important form of Aramaic, known as Mandean, was spoken in Persia by various groups.

Because of the technical character of this subject, only a few examples are appropriate here. The Hebrew verb distinguishes between masculine and feminine: *'azal* = "he went," but *'azelah* = "she went." The feminine ending *-ah* is standard through the Old Testament, but in Deuteronomy 32:36, a poetic passage, the expression "is gone" appears as *'azelat*, preserving the archaic ending *-at*.[15] With regard to syntax, as we will note in chapter 6, in most Old Testament books the so-called imperfect and perfect tenses of Hebrew are not used primarily to indicate the temporal distinctions of past-present-future. In Chronicles, however, this temporal indication becomes prominent. An example from the vocabulary may be especially interesting. The standard Old Testament word for "take" is *lqh*, but this word underwent a semantic shift in the direction of "buy," and so the meaning "take" was appropriated by *ns'* ("carry").[16]

Greek

Our earliest historical evidence for the Greek language consists of some important tablets discovered in Mycene early in the twentieth century, though not deciphered until the 1950s.[17] The language of these documents is a form of Greek spoken at least as far back as the thirteenth century B.C., that is, about half a millennium earlier than our oldest, previously known inscriptions. Mycenean Greek has had an enormous

---

[15]The subject of the verb, "strength," is feminine in Hebrew. For other examples see Eduard Y. Kutscher, *A History of the Hebrew Language*, ed. Raphael Kutscher (Jerusalem: Magnes, and Leiden: Brill, 1982), p. 39.

[16]Kutscher (ibid., p. 83) contrasts 1 Samuel 31:12–13 with 1 Chronicles 10:12, which changes two other words in addition to *lqh*. He also notes that the expression *laqah 'iššah* ("take a wife" = "marry") is changed to *nasa' 'iššah* in Ezra 10:44.

[17]These tablets were not written using the Greek alphabet but a previously unknown script. The exciting story of its decipherment is available in John Chadwick, *The Decipherment of Linear B* (Cambridge: Cambridge University Press, 1958). For the linguistic implications of Mycenean, cf. L. R. Palmer, *The Greek Language* (Atlantic Highlands, N.J.: Humanities Press, 1980), chap. 2.

impact on our understanding of both Aegean prehistory and post-Mycenean dialectal developments.

The reason this material is of such importance is that the Greek language in the classical period was greatly fragmented. Because of geographical distance and the isolation characteristic of the city-states, the dialect spoken by Greeks who lived on the western coast of Asia Minor (Ionia) differed significantly from that spoken in Athens (part of Attica); the differences would have been more noticeable when Ionic was contrasted with Aeolic (spoken in Thessaly and elsewhere), and even more so when contrasted with Doric (spoken in Corinth, for example). These dialects appear to have been mutually intelligible, and the Greeks were very much conscious of their common ethnic identity, but we should not minimize the degree of linguistic diversity that characterized the Greek-speaking world from the time of the earliest inscriptions in the eighth century to the period in which the New Testament was written.

For example, the Greek word for *sea* would have been pronounced *thalassa* in Ionic but *thalatta* in Attic. In both of these dialects the word for *house* was *oikias*, whereas the rest of the Greek dialects pronounced it *woikia*. Most of the Greek dialects used the ending *-men* to indicate that the subject of the verb is the first person plural (e.g., *esthiomen*, "we eat"), while the Dorians preserved the older ending *-mes* (cf. the related Latin ending, as in *amamus*, "we love"). In addition to these and many other phonological and grammatical differences, the vocabulary in each region had its own distinctives.

As is well known, Athens became the cultural center of the Greek-speaking peoples in the classical period. Naturally, the Attic dialect spoken in this city played a special role in literary work. Indeed, most authors (especially if they were writing prose) chose Attic as their primary medium. It may be worthwhile pointing out that among all the Greek dialects Attic was the most "corrupt"—at least if we use this word as many do today when they argue that the English language is being corrupted! The three examples mentioned in the previous paragraph consist of sound *changes* found in Attic but not always in the other dialects. The loss of the *w*-sound, as in *oikia*, was shared by Ionic (a closely related dialect), but not by others, while the sound -*tt*- for -*ss*- was unique to Attic. How corrupt (or dynamic, depending on one's perspective!) Attic must have sounded to other Greek speakers is especially evident in its characteristic vowel contractions. The Ionic -*eo*- combination, for example (as in *kaleomenos*, "called") was "slurred" in Attic to the *u*-sound (*kaloumenos*).[18]

Of course, Attic was neither worse nor better than other dialects, as far as its linguistic structure was concerned. Because it was put to use by brilliant minds, however, this dialect became ideally suited, through a rich vocabulary and a broad stylistic potential, to express in written form the great intellectual flowering of the classical period. As long as we keep in mind that *any* language, spoken by these same intellectuals, would have become ideally suited for the same purpose, we may indeed celebrate the excellence of Attic Greek and its influence in Western civilization.

After the fourth century B.C., and as a result of Alexander the Great's extraordinary conquests, Attic was gradually adopted as a *lingua franca* not only by other Greek speakers but also by the populations of many diverse countries. Inevitably, the language underwent some radical changes in its process of becoming a *koinē dialektos* (the common speech). Many of these changes consisted of simplifications, as in the gradual abandonment of uncommon formations (the verb *deiknymi*, "to show," could now be conjugated as though it belonged to the more usual pattern, *deiknyō*). Following the popular tendency to intensify verbs, the Greeks formed numerous new compounds.

---

[18]To take things a step further: Greek was one of the most "corrupt" Indo-European languages. For example, the initial Indo-European sound *y*- (preserved not only in Sanskrit *yugám* and Latin *iugum* but even in English *yoke*) changed to *z*- in Greek (*zygon*); while initial *s*- became *h*, as in the pronoun *ho* (Sansk. *sá*). This last example is especially interesting to me because in many forms of Spanish (my native language) a comparable sound change, the partial loss of final -*s* (*las casas* becomes *lah casah*), is judged by some to be an ignorant corruption of Castillian. (And, incidentally, Castillian was the most progressive or "corrupt" of all the medieval dialects in Spain!)

The vocabulary was otherwise greatly enriched, often by the adoption of non-Greek words.

Not surprisingly, around New Testament times a reaction to these developments set in. It was indeed claimed by some that the Greek language had degenerated and that it must be restored to its former greatness. Books were written specifying what forms were acceptable—namely, those that could be attested in the writings of the classical period. For example, the lexicographer Phrynichus, who lived in the second century A.D., condemned the verb *eucharistō* (the common New Testament term for "give thanks," still alive and well in Modern Greek) on the grounds that "the approved ones" used the phrase *charin eidenai*.[19] This movement, which came to be known as *Atticism*, succeeded in creating a deep division in the Greek language, so that the speech of the home had to compete with an artificial form (used mainly in writing and formal speech). This infamous "language question" was a basic element in various social and political upheavals in Greece, and it has been only in the last decade or so that the country has enjoyed a measure of linguistic peace.

It is interesting that the language of the New Testament is quite free of the usual Atticizing features. Indeed, some of the books, especially the Gospel of Mark, are written in a very informal, colloquial style, but even the Epistle to the Hebrews, whose author must have had some literary pretensions, avoids the stilted expression that characterized the Atticists. The differences between the language of the New Testament and the Greek used by pagan writers provoked much discussion throughout the history of the church. In the nineteenth century, the view that the New Testament was written in a unique language—heavily semiticized and perhaps made to order by the Holy Spirit—gained in popularity. The discovery in Egypt of thousands of Greek papyri, however, showed that most of the grammatical and lexical peculiarities of the New Testament could be paralleled in documents written by ordinary people for

---

[19]Robert Browning, *Medieval and Modern Greek*, 2d ed. (Cambridge: Cambridge University Press, 1983), p. 47.

day-to-day purposes (family letters, commercial transactions, etc.).

Of special interest in this connection is the influence that Hebrew and Aramaic must have exerted on Palestinian Greek. This influence is most clearly seen in the vocabulary, which changes more quickly and easily than other aspects of language. The most obvious (though also the most superficial) evidence of foreign influence is the phenomenon of loanwords, as when English "borrows" the Spanish word *sombrero* to describe a particular type of hat for which there is no native English term. Several examples of this tendency are found in the Greek New Testament, perhaps the best known being *abba* (the Aramaic word for "father"; cf. Rom. 8:15).

A somewhat different phenomenon consists of so-called loan translations, that is, attempts to translate an idiom or expression by imitating the word-combination of the foreign language. For example, instead of simply borrowing the word *skyscraper*, Spanish speakers tried to reproduce it with the similar combination *rascacielos*. In the same way, the LXX translators took the Hebrew idiom *nasa' panim* ("to lift the face" = "to pay regard to a person, to be partial") and rendered it literally as *prosōpon lambanein* (cf. Gal. 2:6).

Perhaps the most important examples of foreign lexical influence are semantic loans. Instead of borrowing a whole word (a sound combination plus its meaning), speakers who recognize a partial equivalence between a certain native word and the corresponding foreign term may decide, consciously or unconsciously, to "borrow the rest" of the foreign word's meaning—that is, to "extend" the meaning of the native word so that it corresponds more fully to the foreign word. When we say, *I give you my word*, we are using the term *word* in imitation of the French *parole*, with its extended meaning "promise." Some important theological terms in the New Testament reflect a similar development. The Hebrew *kabod* ("weight, honor") is difficult to translate when used to describe a brilliant divine manifestation. Because the Greek *doxa* ("opinion") could be used in the sense of "reputation," the LXX translators chose it to render the Hebrew term and thus the Greek word took on an extra theological nuance, "glory."[20]

It is beyond dispute that most New Testament authors wrote in a style that occasionally reflects their Hebrew/Aramaic background. Moreover, the intellectual and spiritual power of the gospel message would inevitably have left an imprint on the speech of the early Christians, just as it has on the language of modern English-speaking believers. Nevertheless, there is nothing exotic or artificial about New Testament Greek. The apostles were primarily interested in communicating their message clearly and vigorously. And under God's guidance they succeeded.

---

[20]For a more detailed discussion see chap. 3 of my book, *Biblical Words and Their Meaning: An Introduction to Lexical Semantics* (Grand Rapids: Zondervan, 1983). More broadly, on the question of whether New Testament Greek is a unique language, see my article, "Bilingualism and the Character of Palestinian Greek," *Biblica* 61 (1980): 198–219. For a fine study of syntactical influence from Hebrew-Aramaic, see E. C. Maloney, *Semitic Influence in Marcan Syntax* (SBLDS 51; Chico, Calif.: Scholars Press, 1981).

5

DESCRIBING THE BIBLICAL LANGUAGES (I)

In attempting to describe and understand any language, the question soon arises: How shall we slice the pie? Traditionally, a sharp distinction has existed between (1) dictionaries or lexicons, which describe the vocabulary, and (2) grammars, where almost every other aspect of language is treated. Grammar books in turn have been divided into (a) a description of the sounds (*phonology*) and writing of the language; (b) an analysis of the rules for word formation and inflection (*morphology* or *accidence*); and (c) a more substantive section dealing with *syntax*, that is, the arrangement of words to form phrases and sentences, along with their resultant meaning.

The boundaries dividing these areas are not always clear, and inconsistencies often develop. Contemporary linguists, influenced primarily by so-called transformational grammar, add a fourth category, *semantics*. A recent textbook, for example, outlines as follows the sets of rules involved in language acquisition:

(i) a set of *syntactic* rules which specify how sentences are built up out of phrases, and phrases out of words

(ii) a set of *morphological* rules which specify how words are built up out of morphemes (i.e., grammatical units smaller than the word)

77

(iii)   a set of *phonological* rules which specify how words, phrases, and sentences are pronounced

(iv)   a set of *semantic* rules which specify how words, phrases, and sentences are interpreted (i.e., what their meaning is)[1]

For our purposes—which do not really include the teaching of grammar—a less popular, but pedagogically more useful, classification will serve just as well.[2] Based on those units of language that are quickly recognized by all speakers, our outline will focus successively on (1) sounds = phonology, (2) words = lexicology, (3) phrases and sentences = syntax, and (4) paragraphs and larger units = discourse and genre analysis. Each of the last three items will be further subdivided into matters of form (morphology in the broad sense) and meaning (semantics).

SOUNDS

Since neither Hellenistic Greek nor the Hebrew of ancient Israel is spoken today—and since the tape recordings that were produced in the ancient world are of notoriously poor quality— modern phonologists are somewhat handicapped when they seek to analyze the sound systems of the biblical languages. Moreover, only very rarely do phonological questions have a direct bearing on the interpretation of texts. For these reasons, we need not devote much attention to the sounds of ancient Greek and Hebrew/Aramaic in this book.[3] On the other hand, it would be a mistake to ignore phonology altogether. In the first place, we do know a great deal—if not as much as we would like about ancient sounds, and especially about the structural significance of those sounds in their respective languages.

[1]Andrew Radford, *Transformational Grammar: A First Course* (CTL; Cambridge: Cambridge University Press, 1988), pp. 18–19.

[2]This approach, which has not caught on, was suggested (excluding the attention to paragraphs) many years ago by J. Ries and commended by Ullmann, *Principles*, pp. 26, 32–36 (note the diagram on p. 39).

[3]For a useful integration of modern phonology and Ancient Greek, see David A. Black, *Linguistics for Students of New Testament Greek: A Survey of Basic Concepts and Applications* (Grand Rapids: Baker, 1988), chap. 2.

Second, there is no better way to understand what modern linguistics is all about than by seeing this discipline operate on sound systems: phonological structures are small (often thirty to forty significant sounds) and consist of relatively simple relationships, so that linguistic analysis becomes clearer and firmer than it is when dealing with the other, more complex aspects of language. In the third place, some familiarity with the phonology of Greek and Hebrew provides a base on which to build an accurate knowledge of the biblical languages as a whole; indeed, certain kinds of interpretive questions, though not directly affected by phonology, can be answered more reliably if the interpreter has a good grasp of linguistic structure (of which sounds are a part).

Probably the most elementary principle of phonology is *the need to distinguish between letters and sounds*. This distinction could be viewed as a restatement (or at least a specific example) of the principle that, in linguistic study, oral language takes precedence over its written expression. In our modern society, where the written form has such a strong cultural significance, we tend to confuse these elements. Moreover, since we cannot study Greek and Hebrew by interviewing ancient speakers, we are confined to literary remains, and that factor tends to blur distinctions even further.

The point at issue here is that alphabets are only *approximations* of sound inventories. When the alphabet was first devised—probably by Northwest Semites no later than 1500 B.C.—it presumably corresponded quite closely to the set of significant sounds used by the language in question. As that language (as well as its relatives, such as Hebrew, which used the same alphabet) developed, the written system could not easily keep up with gradual changes in the phonology. The problem was further complicated when that alphabet was adopted by unrelated languages, such as Greek.[4] In any case, sound and writing move almost inexorably farther and farther

---

[4]See Joseph Naveh, *Early History of the Alphabet: An Introduction to West Semitic Epigraphy and Palaeography* (Jerusalem: Magnes, and Leiden: Brill, 1982), which includes a chapter on the Greek alphabet.

apart. Languages that have experienced very rapid phonological changes (e.g., French and English) end up with a significant disparity between sounds and alphabet. To dramatize the problem, Bernard Shaw once pointed out, somewhat unfairly to be sure, that in English it is possible to spell the word *fish* with the letter sequence *ghoti*.[5]

Now as we noticed in the previous chapter, Hebrew and its cognate languages depend heavily on their consonantal system and only secondarily on the vowels. Prior to the Middle Ages, in fact, all Hebrew writing was done exclusively with consonants (though a few of the consonants could serve to indicate vowel sounds in some instances of ambiguity). Jewish medieval scholars responsible for the transmission of the Hebrew Scriptures—these scribes were known as *Masoretes*, "transmitters"—developed a sophisticated system of notation to indicate not only the vowels but also almost every phonetic variation imaginable. Their purpose was not primarily linguistic: they were interested in preserving as carefully as possible, now that Hebrew was no longer a living tongue, the precise way in which the Bible was read (and cantillated—that is, chanted in the synagogue services).

As a result, modern seminarians who undertake the study of the Hebrew Bible are confronted with a bewildering number of signs. Many of these signs (especially the "accents" used for cantillation) are usually ignored, but that still leaves some complications. Textbooks, unfortunately, seldom make clear to the student that most of those notations have little linguistic significance. For example, as soon as students are introduced to the alphabet, they note that a few of the consonants can be pronounced in two different ways, depending on whether or not they have a dot (the *dagesh*) in the middle. Thus students are usually taught to pronounce the letter *dalet* like the English *d* if it has that dot (דּ), but like *th* as in *them* if it does not (ד). Strictly speaking, that distinction is merely *phonetic*, not *phonemic*, because it cannot be used to distinguish between words. Speakers of ancient Hebrew were probably quite unaware of the

---

[5]Pronounce the *gh* as in *tough*, the *o* as in *women*, and the *ti* as in *nation*.

distinction, much as modern speakers of Spanish are unaware of a similar distinction in their pronunciation of the two *d*'s in the word *soldado* ("soldier"; the last syllable is pronounced roughly like English *though*).[6]

Another example of the same class is the large number of vowel signs used by the Masoretes. How many actual *phonemes* (belonging to any given chronological stage) were represented by these signs is a matter of debate, but we may be sure that there was no one-to-one correspondence.[7] Modern seminarians, however, tend to identify all the written vowel signs as significant sounds; and while this mistake may not affect adversely the doctrinal content of their future sermons, they go through a period of unnecessary confusion that affects their perception of the language as a whole. This problem is further aggravated by the fact that most grammars seek to describe the Masoretic vowels through diachronic and comparative data.

Sound values are a little easier in the case of New Testament Greek, but here too misunderstandings are not uncommon. The problem begins as soon as students are required to attach an English sound to each Greek letter. The "classroom" pronunciation of Greek in America (and, *mutatis mutandis*, in most European countries) is quite odd and artificial: it mixes sounds from various stages in the evolution of the language and creates a couple of new ones! Our task is made harder by the fact that the New Testament was written at a time when important phonological changes were taking place—no

---

[6] I mention this item from personal experience. Though Spanish is my native language, it never occurred to me that I pronounced the *d* (as well as *b* and *g*) in two different ways—until my early twenties, when I began the study of Hebrew! The rule, for both Hebrew and Spanish, is that the consonants in question are *spirantized* (the breath is not blocked by the tongue [or lips or glottis] but allowed to flow) when they follow a vowel sound. Thus the *d* and *th* sounds are said to be *allophones* of the one *phoneme* /d/: which of the two is used is determined by the sound context, not by a desire of the speaker to distinguish meaning. Allophones therefore are found in "complementary distribution" and cannot be linguistically contrasted; they do not play a role in the phonological structure of the language.

[7] Some estimates put the number of vocalic phonemes as low as five; see Kutscher, *History*, p. 29.

doubt at different rates and in different ways from region to region. The differences between Classical Greek (say, in fifth-century B.C. Athens) and Medieval Greek are many. The most striking change is in the vowels. Ancient Greek had, aside from the diphthongs, a set of ten phonemes:

> long and short[8] α
> long and short ι
> long and short υ
> long η and short ε
> long ω and short o

By the Middle Ages, however, many of these sounds had merged; indeed, all of the following are today pronounced the same way (like English *ee*): ι, η, υ, $\varepsilon\iota$, $o\iota$.

The question then becomes: Where does the New Testament language belong in this process? Precision eludes us. The initial breakdown of the vowel system can be traced as far back as the fourth century B.C.,[9] but we cannot be sure how many changes had taken place by the first century. Ancient writings of an informal nature (especially graffiti) can be especially helpful to the linguist, since people often violate spelling conventions by writing as they speak. For example, the Greek word for "rod," $\dot{\rho}\alpha\beta\delta o\varsigma$ (rhabdos), has been attested with the spelling $\rho\alpha\upsilon\delta o\varsigma$ as early as the New Testament period. It is therefore clear that already at that time (1) the sound represented by β had shifted from the occlusive [b], in which the air

---

[8]The words "long" and "short" here mean exactly what they say. Unlike the English vowels often described as long, which are really diphthongs (e.g., the *a* in *cake*, where the quality of the vowel changes during its pronunciation), vowels in Ancient Greek, as well as in many other languages, could be pronounced for a duration of what we may call one unit of time or for a duration of two units (that is, twice as long), but without a change in the quality of the vowel. Such a distinction seems overly subtle to English speakers, yet in Arabic (to use the classic example) the difference between *jamāl* and *jamal* is that between "beauty" and "camel."

[9]According to the researches of Sven-Tage Teodorsson, *The Phonemic System of the Attic Dialect 400/340 B.C.* (Studia graeca et latina gathoburgensia 32; Lund: Berlingska Boytryckeriet, 1974), cf. also *The Phonology of Ptolemaic Greek* (Studia 36; 1977) and *The Phonology of Attic in the Hellenistic Period* (Studia 40; 1978).

is stopped momentarily, to a sound that allowed the air to flow freely; and (2) the diphthong αυ had shifted to a sound approaching that of the English combination *av*.[10]

It is useful to keep in mind that certain features of Hellenistic Greek are remnants of previous centuries. Students learn early on in their study of Greek, for instance, that the preposition ἀπό (*apo*, "from") drops the last vowel if the next word begins with a vowel (ἀπ' ἀρχῆς). Moreover, if that next word begins with a vowel that has the rough breathing mark, a further change takes place, as in ἀφ' ὑμῶν (*aph' hymōn*, "from you"). By New Testament times the letter φ was probably already pronounced [f], and there would seem to be no reason why the sound [p] should change to [f] just because the following word begins with the sound [h]. In the classical period, however, the φ was pronounced [pʰ],[11] so one can easily understand how the sequence *ap hymōn* would lead to a spelling representing *apʰ hymōn*.

The attentive reader may have noticed that in my effort to describe the state of the sound system of Greek in the first century (synchronic linguistics), I have been compelled to take into account historical (diachronic) data. Because of our limited information, this problem is inevitable and shows that the two perspectives, while distinct, are not totally separable. Using them to supplement each other, however, is not the same as *confusing* them. The key is to avoid our tendency to explain synchrony by means of diachrony, as though one could read the linguistic realities of an earlier period into the state of the language we are concerned with.

---

[10] In Modern Greek β is pronounced like English *v*, while αυ and ευ are pronounced *av* and *ev* (or, before certain consonants, *af, ef*). For details see especially Peter Mackridge, *The Modern Greek Language: A Descriptive Analysis of Standard Modern Greek* (Oxford: Oxford University Press, 1985).

[11] The reader should recall, from the discussion in chap. 2, that the sound represented by English *p* is in fact an aspirate very much like Ancient Greek φ; the unaspirated *p* of French and Spanish (but also of English in such words as *spot*) corresponds to Greek π. Thus Ancient Greek had two distinct phonemes for what in English is one phoneme (with two allophones). The situation is similar with the pairs τ/θ and κ/χ.

WORDS

Form

Just as we can distinguish phonemes (linguistically meaningful sounds) from those variations (allophones) that do not affect the structure of the system, so can we distinguish *morphemes* from *allomorphs*. Like phonemes, morphemes are minimal units; unlike phonemes, which do not by themselves convey meaning, morphemes have semantic content. For example, the unit *cat* happens to be a complete word, but because it cannot be further subdivided it is also a morpheme. We can, however, add the morpheme *-s*, which has the semantic content of plurality, to form the "new" word *cats* (composed of two morphemes). The morpheme of plurality, though, can be "realized" in more than one way, leading to a variety of allomorphs: compare the different pronunciation of this morpheme in *cats, boys,* and *boxes.*

The rules for formal changes in words differ significantly among languages. Chinese, for example, is characterized by a large number of monosyllabic words that do not change in form. Turkish, on the other hand, takes a base word and adds not one but several morphemes at the end:

ev = "house"
evler = "houses"
evleri = "his houses"
evlerinden = "from his houses"[12]

In contrast to both of these types, the biblical languages are *inflecting* in character, that is, they modify a part of the word (usually the ending) to express various relationships. English in its early history was primarily inflecting, but in its modern dress it retains few inflections (the plural morpheme mentioned above, the past *-ed* ending, the possessive *-'s*, etc.). Hebrew and

---

[12]The example is taken (in simplified form) from John Lyons, *Introduction to Theoretical Linguistics* (Cambridge: Cambridge University Press, 1969), p. 188. This feature of Turkish, shared by some other languages, is what motivated the description *agglutinative.*

Aramaic have retained a larger proportion of inflecting features, and Greek even more.

For example, the only inflections allowed by most English nouns are those of plurality and possession, though the personal pronouns have also retained the so-called accusative case (*him, her, them*), indicating the object of the verb. In addition to features comparable to those three forms (each of which, incidentally, serves a variety of purposes), Greek adds a fourth, called dative, usually to indicate the indirect object of the verb, and a fifth, the vocative (more restricted in use). Hebrew and Aramaic lost the nominal inflections,[13] except those indicating plurality. Adjectives, however, can be inflected to indicate gender (as can Greek adjectives), something unknown in English: the word *tall* does not change at all, regardless of the kind of noun it modifies (contrast Spanish, *el hombre alto*, "the tall man," but *la mujer alta*, "the tall woman").[14]

The richness of Greek inflections is especially apparent in the verbal conjugations. While English has retained only one inflectional morpheme to indicate the category of person,[15] Greek and Hebrew, along with many other languages, have six: first, second, and third persons, each singular and plural. While English has only one morpheme to indicate tense (*-ed*, simple past), Greek has a variety of forms, each of which is combined with the indicator of person:

> *pempō*, "I send"; *pempomen*, "we send"
> *pempsō*, "I will send"; *pempsomen*, "we will send"
> *epempon*, "I was sending"; *epempomen*, "we were sending"
> *epempsa*, "I sent"; *epempsamen*, "we sent"
> etc.

---

[13]Proto-Semitic had three nominal inflexions, still preserved in Arabic. As we will see, there is a relationship between the presence/absence of case endings and the question of word order in a sentence.

[14]It should be noted, incidentally, that these inflectional endings, though applauded by some admirers of the classical languages, add absolutely nothing to what the speaker wants to say. One could just as easily argue that English, by wisely dropping these changes, is a model of linguistic economy and thus saves its speakers a great deal of mental energy!

[15]The ending *-s* for the third person singular in the present tense: *I come*, but *he/she/it comes.*

Although Hebrew does not have as many tenses, it goes Greek one better by including gender in its inflections:

> *malak*, "he reigned"; *malekah*, "she reigned"
> *yimlok*, "he will reign"; *timlok*, "she will reign"
> etc.

We could devote much more space to the intricacies of lexical morphology.[16] One other item, however, may be worth mentioning here, and that is the ease with which Greek forms compounds. Every speaker of English is familiar with the process: we may, for example, prefix the adjective *counter* to other adjectives or nouns, such as *attack, culture, revolutionary*, etc., and thus create new words. This process is much more productive in such a language as German, whose speakers coin numerous words every day, especially by combining prepositions with nouns and verbs. Similarly, a Greek speaker could easily take the verb *dechomai* ("take, receive, await"), then prefix a preposition to form *ekdechomai* ("take from"), then further "strengthen" the verb by prefixing another preposition to form *apekdechomai* ("to await eagerly"). As a result, many Greek words are "transparent"; that is, the reader can readily identify their components and thus infer their approximate meaning. Hebrew, on the other hand, does not lend itself easily to this kind of word formation; but as we saw in the previous chapter, the Semitic languages can generate a large number of forms by means of verbal stems.

Meaning

The study of meaning encompasses a broad and bewildering range of subjects. For the moment we are concerned only with word-meaning or lexical semantics, a topic that attracts great popular interest and, partly for that very reason, is susceptible to much misunderstanding. As will become clear, separating lexical semantics from other aspects of meaning is

---

[16]For a clear discussion of Greek morphology, see Black, *Linguistics*, chap. 3. The morphology of biblical Hebrew is summarized in Kutscher, *History*, pp. 30–43.

somewhat artificial, but this procedure can provide the foundation for subsequent discussion.[17]

ETYMOLOGY

Perhaps no aspect of language study proves more fascinating than tracing the development of word meanings. Who can resist the charm of finding out that the word *gossip* comes from *godsib* ("related to God"), used of godparents in the Middle Ages, and that the current meaning of the word arose from the chatter—not always edifying—typical at christenings in those days? This kind of information can shed much light on the workings of language as well as on society.[18] For some reason, however, most of us go on to infer that such a discovery gives us a better understanding of the *present* meaning of the word. And that is where our troubles begin.

The distinction between synchrony and diachrony is nowhere more relevant than in our study of lexical semantics. It should be quite apparent that the vast majority of English speakers today, being quite unaware of the history behind *gossip*, use the word without any reference to christenings, the concept of godparenting, or anything of the sort. Imagine, then, the following conversation between Harry and Mike:

"Say, Mike, I heard some interesting gossip at the convention last week."

"Oh, really? Who was being christened?"

"Nobody was being christened. Why do you ask?"

"Come on, Harry! The basic meaning of the word *gossip* has to do with godparenting."

---

[17]What follows summarizes most of the principles covered in my book, *Biblical Words*, to which the reader is referred for fuller documentation and detail. The recent and successful work by Peter Cotterell and Max Turner, *Linguistics and Biblical Interpretation* (Downers Grove, Ill.: InterVarsity, 1989), includes a substantive chapter on lexical semantics that I heartily recommend. Note also D. A. Cruse, *Lexical Semantics* (CTL; Cambridge: Cambridge University Press, 1986).

[18]See especially the literate discussion of the social dimensions of semantic change by Geoffrey Hughes, *Words in Time: The Social History of English Vocabulary* (New York: Blackwell, 1988).

"Who cares? I was just talking about the rumors I heard last week."

"That's what you think. Words preserve their core meanings, so it's impossible to understand your statement without some reference to christening."

"Take my word for it, Mike: I did not intend to say anything at all about christenings or godparents."

"But you can't just make language mean what you want it to. Seems like you would have more respect for the essence of language. I'm rather disappointed in you."

Such a conversation sounds ludicrous, and indeed none of us goes around injecting historical ideas of that sort into statements made by our friends. When it comes to literature, however, especially older literature, this method of interpretation becomes the order of the day—and, unlike Harry, the apostle Paul is not here to defend himself. As mentioned in the previous chapter, there are occasions (as in some poetic passages of the Old Testament) when we come across rare words whose meaning is unclear and for which etymological analysis can provide some help. Most words, however, are widely attested and their meaning can be clearly established from the numerous contexts in which they appear. This state of affairs is especially true of New Testament Greek, which ironically has been subjected to a great deal of (unneeded) etymologizing.

One of the reasons etymologies have become popular is that they provide interesting illustrations. A preacher, for example, may feel that his sermon is more concrete if he tells the congregation that the "basic meaning" of the Greek word for truth, *alētheia*, is "unhiddenness," or that the "real point" of sin, *hamartia*, is "missing the mark." Certainly the idea of "release upward from a binding contract" as the meaning of Greek *analysis* is much more exciting than the simple translation "departure."[19] Even more productive of sermon illustrations is what may be called "reverse etymologizing," as when we are told, on the basis of the verb *metamorphoō* ("transform," Rom. 12:2), that sanctification is like the process of change from a

---

[19]See above, chap. 1, p. 14.

chrysalis to a butterfly. The use of English *metamorphosis* as a technical term to describe this process, however, is a modern peculiarity, and there is no reason to think that Paul had such a biological thought in mind when he penned those words.

Perhaps there is no harm done by using etymological information for illustrative purposes, as long as the person doing so and the audience that hears it are clear on what is happening. For exegetical purposes, however, our guiding principle ought to be, What did the author have in mind to say? And since authors cannot have in mind what they and their audiences are unaware of, etymology seldom has a role to play in the interpretation of texts. Other factors must be brought to bear, and we will consider these now.

REFERENCE AND STRUCTURE

As children grow up, they often learn the meaning of a new word by the parents' pointing to an object and pronouncing the word in question: "Look out the window, Karen; that's a *cow*." If the needed object is not readily available for pointing, the next best method—not fundamentally different from pointing—is to give a description: "A cow is like a puppy, only much bigger, has horns, and goes 'Moooo.'" Even as adults, we partly build up our vocabulary in a similar way.

Almost inevitably, we tend to think of meaning as a one-to-one correspondence between an object in the world (the extralinguistic referent) and the word that refers to it. This way of looking at meaning seems to work much of the time, but careful reflection makes clear that, by itself, it is a rather unsatisfactory explanation. To begin with, children learn the most basic and frequent words in their language without any pointing or description. This is true not only of what we may call "function words," such as articles and prepositions (which act primarily as grammatical markers); it also applies to many verbs, abstract nouns, etc.

More to the point, both children and adults build up *most* of their vocabulary simply by hearing (or reading) words used in a variety of contexts. Much of this learning is unconscious. While reading a magazine article, we come across a word we haven't really seen before; without even noticing that it is a "new" word, we manage to infer its meaning, more or less automatically, from the whole context. This fact demonstrates that word meaning is not only—and perhaps not primarily—a matter of *reference*, of linking up words with objects outside of language.[20] To a large extent, word meaning is constituted by the relationships that exist *within language itself.*

Just as English-speaking children intuitively figure out (through gradual familiarity with phonological relations) that the [t] in *stop* and the [tʰ] in *top* are alternate sounds of the one phoneme /t/, and that this phoneme is quite a different one from the very similar /d/, so do they learn the "value" and therefore proper use of words by ascertaining their contrasts and combinations, in short, by mastering lexical *structure.* Consider this sentence: *Some tall men ate slowly.* We could say that the meaning of *some* is largely determined by its contrast with other words that can occupy the same slot in that sentence, for example, *the, few, several, many* (similarly, *tall* contrasts with *short, thin, fat,* etc.; *men* with *women, boys*; and so on).[21] Each of these words occupies a segment out of a larger field of meaning, and the presence of other words in the same field affects its value. Suppose, for example, that the word *several* were to disappear from the language without a new word taking its place; in that case, *some* or *few* (or both) would have to occupy

---

[20] My comments here are not intended to prejudice the larger questions involved in evaluating "the reference theory of meaning." One may downplay the role of reference in *lexical* meaning without suggesting that the concept of reference as such is invalid or inappropriate. In particular, I would want to argue that the reference theory accounts satisfactorily (if not exhaustively) for *propositions,* such as those involved in historical narratives. Cotterell and Turner have an excellent, balanced discussion of this subject in *Linguistics,* pp. 82–90.

[21] These contrasting relationships are technically known as *paradigmatic,* a term used in phonology to indicate the contrast among similar phonemes, such as /b/, /v/, /p/, /f/. The term *syntagmatic* is used to describe the possible combinations into which phonemes can enter, such as /t/-/o/-/p/ in the word *top.* Note that certain combinations, such as /o/-/t/-/p/, are not permissible in English; similarly, English rules do not permit beginning a word with the sound represented by *ng* (as in *-ing*), even though that combination is common in some languages, as in the African name, (Lake) Ngami.

the area vacated by *several*. In short, the range of meaning, and therefore the potential sentence use, of a word is established by its opposition to semantically neighboring words.

But "range of meaning" and "potential use" are vague concepts. What really matters is what happens when words are combined with each other in specific *contexts*. The rules of English do not allow for certain combinations, such as *Slowly men ate tall*. Words that are similar in meaning (synonyms) are often distinguished simply by the contexts in which they can occur: the expressions *deep thinker* and *profound thinker* are almost interchangeable, but whereas *deep water* is common enough, *profound water* is regarded as unacceptable. Accordingly, one should treat with healthy skepticism discussions of biblical synonyms that fail to indicate the specific contexts in which the supposed similarities and differences among the words occur.

We may illustrate how structural relations function in the biblical vocabulary by citing a specific application that has become well known.[22] The terms "image" and "likeness" (Hebrew *ṣelem* and *demut*) in Genesis 1:26 have caused heated debate among scholars. Much of the disagreement, however, arises out of the assumption that the terms are primarily (or exclusively) referential and that by focusing on each word we can "squeeze from it alone a decisive oracle about its meaning." Instead, Barr proposes to "look at a whole group of words and hope that meaning may be indicated by the choice of one word rather than another within this group." The results of Barr's research are that *ṣelem* was probably chosen because, though somewhat ambiguous, it was the term least likely to be misunderstood. The addition of *demut* then helped to circumscribe its meaning "by indicating that the sense intended for *ṣelem* must lie within that part of its range which overlaps with the range of *demut*."

A significant advance in biblical lexicology is the recent publication of the United Bible Societies' dictionary of New

---

[22]James Barr, "The Image of God in the Book of Genesis—A Study of Terminology," *BJRL* 51 (1968–69): 11–26; quotations from pp. 14–15, 24.

Testament Greek, prepared according to structural relations.[23] By using this tool, students can develop valuable sensitivity to the makeup of the Greek vocabulary generally, as opposed to the tunnel-vision characteristic of much word study. In this dictionary, words are not arranged alphabetically (the index is the place for that) but according to semantic fields or domains. At a glance, the user can see the various choices (that is, the lexical contrasts) available to the New Testament writers when they sought to express an idea. By focusing on groups of words rather than on isolated items, biblical interpreters can analyze the text with greater reliability.

Suppose that we are studying Paul's letter to the Philippians and become intrigued by 1:3–4: "I thank my God every time I remember you. In all my prayers for all of you, I always pray with joy." A more literal translation would read, "I thank [*eucharistō*] my God upon every remembrance of you always in every prayer [*deēsei*] of mine for all of you with joy making the prayer [*tēn deēsin poioumenos*]." Apart from some syntactical questions in this passage, we may wonder what is the precise meaning of the noun *deēsis*. If we check the index of the UBS *Lexicon*, we find that only one meaning ("plea") is assigned to this word and that it is treated in section 33 (terms dealing with communication), subsection L (general meaning "ask for, request"). This subsection, however, includes more than a dozen additional terms that belong to the same area of meaning (semantic domain); moreover, we notice that subsection M includes terms with the more specific meaning "pray."

As we compare these various terms and check them more carefully, we discover some interesting facts, such as the preference in the Gospel of John for common words that have no distinct religious nuance (e.g., *aiteō* and *erōtaō*). In some passages there seems to be a clear distinction between *proseuchē*/*proseuchomai* as general terms and *deēsis*/*deomai* as specific: ". . . always in my prayers [*proseuchēn*] asking [*deome-*

---

[23]Johannes P. Louw and Eugene A. Nida, eds., *Greek-English Lexicon of the New Testament Based on Semantic Domains*, 2 vols. (New York: United Bible Societies, 1988). Cf. my review in *WTJ* 51 (1989): 163–67.

nos] . . ." (Rom. 1:10, literal translation). It would be misleading, however, to apply this distinction everywhere.[24] In Philippians 1:3–4, for example, Paul appears to include the giving of thanks (not only the petitions) under *deēsis*; that is, in this particular context *proseuchē* could have been substituted without any loss of meaning. Similarly, we could argue that in Philippians 4:6, where both of these terms are used, no special distinction is intended;[25] rather, Paul is probably exploiting their similarity to strengthen the stylistic force of his exhortation.

We may be sure that a greater emphasis on the vocabulary as a whole—and a corresponding downplaying of etymological study of individual words by themselves—will lead to responsible exegesis. There is, however, one additional matter that requires our attention.

AMBIGUITY

One often hears complaints about the supposed lack of precision in English. A preacher will say: "We use the word *love* in too many ways: we love God, we love children, we love our work, we even love chocolate. In contrast, the Greeks were very precise in their use of three distinct words for 'love.'" Comments of that sort romanticize Ancient Greek by failing to appreciate the character of language. To begin with, modern English probably has a greater number of words for "love" (both nouns and verbs) than Greek ever did: *affection, devotion, fondness, amorousness, adore, cherish, dote on,* etc., etc.

But even that consideration misses the important point

---

[24]The principle of *neutralization* cuts across all levels of language. Cf. my *Biblical Words*, pp. 165–66. See also David Sankoff, "Sociolinguistics and Syntactic Variation," *LTCS* 4:140–61, especially p. 153: "While it is indisputable that some difference in connotation may, *upon reflection*, be postulated among so-called synonyms whether in isolation or in context, and that in the case of each one a number of competing syntactic constructions may be acceptable in somewhat different contexts, there is no reason to expect these differences to be pertinent every time one of the variant forms is used."

[25]If *proseuchē* is the general term, then it surely includes "petition" as part of its meaning; and if *deēsis* merely means "petition," the inclusion of this term would add no semantic content to the sentence. Cf. my *Philippians* (WEC; Chicago: Moody, 1988), pp. 49–50, 227.

that ambiguity is a valuable and even necessary aspect of all languages, since otherwise the number of words in everyone's active vocabulary would grow to unmanageable proportions. A very high percentage of words in English do double or triple duty, and it is not uncommon to find words that can be assigned half a dozen meanings. A few words even seem to be out of control: the verb *run*, for instance (even after excluding such phrasal constructions as *run against, run in*, etc.), has well over fifty "dictionary" meanings. In spite of this apparent confusion, however, we are rarely stumped by it. Can we even remember when was the last time we failed to grasp a specific use of *run*?

The reason ambiguity is seldom a problem in communication is that the context almost always excludes irrelevant meanings. The context may consist simply of the immediate word linkage: the combination *run an advertisement*, for example, instantly eliminates intransitive meanings (such as "take part in a race") as well as transitive meanings that do not fit that combination (e.g., "accomplish," as in *run errands*; "operate," as in *run the computer*; "cause to crash," as in *run the car into the wall*). Or the context may consist of the subject matter: *He listed the names of the characters* is, in isolation, an ambiguous sentence, since the word combination here allows for a reference to either the names of letters in an alphabet or the names of persons portrayed in a play; the obscurity disappears, however, if we know the sentence was spoken by someone lecturing on Shakespeare. Again, the context may consist of the broad setting in which a sentence was spoken or written: *He brought a suit* has a simple, unequivocal meaning in a laundry shop, but quite a different one in a court of law.

Ambiguity arises more frequently when we read literature distant in time and culture from us, since we are less familiar with the whole context in which the writing originated. Scholars have debated whether Galatians 3:4 should be translated, "Did you suffer so many things in vain?" or "Did you experience so many things [= spiritual blessings] in vain?" The Greek word in question, *paschō*, usually has the negative meaning "suffer," but occasionally it may be used when describing a neutral or even positive experience. The immediate context suggests a positive reference, but if Paul was aware that the Galatians had gone through much suffering, that broader context may have determined the meaning of the verb at 3:4. It is difficult to reach a definitive conclusion.[26]

The fact that we occasionally meet such examples of unintentional ambiguity should not lead us to exaggerate the problem. In particular, we ought to resist the temptation to come up with new, but unattested, meanings that *might* fit the context. A recent article proposed that the use of the Greek words *peritomē* ("circumcision") and *akrobystia* ("uncircumcision") in the New Testament reflects an ethnic slur, that is, "epithets hurled at Gentiles and at Jews respectively by members of the opposite group in Rome and elsewhere."[27] According to this view, *peritomē* should be translated concretely, "circumcised penis" (and *akrobystia* should be translated literally, "foreskin").

All of the evidence for this view, however, is indirect in nature. Indeed, the only unambiguous evidence the author can offer is not from Greek at all but from the corresponding Hebrew word *milah*—and even that from rabbinic writings produced much later than the New Testament. Without explicit information that in fact Gentiles used to throw this kind of insult at Jews, we would need a few examples of *peritomē* where the new proposed meaning is the only one that makes sense.[28] In other words, the reality of lexical ambiguity cannot become a pretext for overworked imagination.

---

[26]For a more extensive discussion of this passage, see my *Biblical Words*, pp. 153–56.

[27]Joel Marcus, "The Circumcision and the Uncircumcision in Rome," *NTS* 35 (1989): 67–81, esp. p. 79.

[28]In the case of rare words or poorly attested literature, we sometimes may need to be satisfied with a less rigorous criterion. In the case of abundantly attested words, however, it is an elementary lexicographical principle that a proposed new meaning that happens to make sense in some contexts cannot be established as long as the attested meanings also make sense. One must offer examples where the alternate meanings do not work. Indeed, Marcus himself (ibid., p. 75) recognizes that there are some passages in Paul where the usual translation is the only one that is possible.

Quite different is the problem we face when a writer is deliberately ambiguous. We rarely come across deliberate ambiguity in normal prose writing, since authors write to be understood. For literary effect, however, authors sometimes tease their readers with double meanings, as when the Gospel of John 1:5 tells us that the darkness did not understand the light; since the Greek verb (katalambanō) can also mean "overcome," quite possibly John has deliberately used an ambiguous word. Before drawing such a conclusion, however, one should have fairly strong contextual reasons. In the case of the Gospel of John, the character of the book as a whole and other likely instances of ambiguity support the conclusion.[29]

More often, deliberate ambiguity arises in poetry, and there are many examples of this in the Old Testament. To be sure, we should not assume that this technique was as important to the psalmists as it seems to be to some modern poets. The evocative features of language, however, do play a significant role in Hebrew poetry. This is especially true of metaphorical language, which has a greater emotional impact on the reader than bare description has. For the psalmist to say that the Lord is his shepherd creates some ambiguity, since the reader is expected to identify the point of comparison between God and a shepherd. The psalmist does resolve the ambiguity when he adds, "I shall not want": clearly, the point of comparison is that the shepherd provides fully for the needs of his sheep. But there remains a measure of ambiguity (richness?) in that the reader can fill in the details, and the psalmist himself goes on to give some instances of the divine provision he has in mind.

Sometimes the ambiguity is more difficult to resolve. After God warns Isaiah about the spiritual callousness of Israel, the prophet asks how long that obduracy will continue. God responds: "Until the cities lie ruined and without inhabitant" (Isa. 6:11). At the end of the passage, however, we read:

---

[29]A similar case can be made for the language of Ezekiel. Cf. Daniel I. Block, "The Prophet of the Spirit: The Use of rwḥ in the Book of Ezekiel," *JETS* 32 (1989): 27–49.

> But as the terebinth and oak
>   leave stumps when they are cut down,
>   so the holy seed will be the stump in the land. (v. 13)

Clearly, the word *stump* is used figuratively for a residue of God's people, but the point of comparison is not obvious, even though the context suggests a hopeful note. By the time we get to chapter 11, however, the obscurity is removed:

> A shoot will come up from the stump of Jesse;
>   from his roots a Branch will bear fruit.
> The Spirit of the LORD will rest on him . . .
> and he will delight in the fear of the LORD. (vv. 1–3)

God will leave a holy remnant among his people, out of whom the Messiah will arise and bring salvation to them.

It is clear, then, that even in poetic passages where the author wishes to exploit the ambiguity of language, the purpose is not at all to confuse but to impress on our hearts the force of the divine message.

6
DESCRIBING THE BIBLICAL LANGUAGES (II)

SENTENCES

In the previous section I proposed to deal with words as individual items, more or less in isolation from sentences. The reader must have noticed, however, that it was impossible to carry through with that proposal. Apart from a few interjections (e.g., *Ouch!*) and simple imperatives (*Come!*), words are not normally used by themselves to communicate what we mean. Evangelicals often stress the view that biblical revelation is *propositional*, that is, it does not consist merely in a vague (and contentless) relationship between God and human beings. This concern, which involves a very important theological truth, acknowledges that the *meaning* of Scripture is to be found in its propositions, not in isolated words. Thus what really matters about the Bible is not just the fact that it contains, say, the verb *sin*, but that it communicates such statements as *All have sinned* (Rom. 3:23).

Not all word-combinations, of course, are sentences in the strict sense of the term. Some combinations are very difficult to distinguish in function from individual words. The meaning of such idioms as *a pain in the neck* cannot really be derived by adding up its parts: the whole combination stands for a simple concept comparable to that of *nuisance*. That is the reason good dictionaries do not merely give the meanings of an individual word: they go on to specify the sense of peculiar combinations in which that word may be found.

Other combinations consist of normal phrases, such as *the brown house, very likely, through the woods,* and so on. We use the term *clause* to describe word combinations that, while seemingly more "important" than phrases because they include a subject and a predicate,[1] may themselves be part of, and even dependent on, a larger utterance; for example, *if they arrive in time,* or *after she ate her lunch.* Full, independent sentences can be quite short: *John arrived.* In languages (including Greek and Hebrew) that incorporate the subject in the verbal form, a single verb can constitute a complete sentence. Sentences can become extremely long and complex, however. Modern English versions may not show it, but Ephesians 1:3–11 consists of one sentence, made up of many shorter sentences and clauses.

Since we are interested in what is usually called *syntax,* this section will not be restricted to full sentences. Phrases and clauses will come under purview as well. On the other hand, we will not be concerned here with complex sentences: the linking together of sentences brings us close to the area of paragraphs and is best considered in the next section. In any case, the boundaries between the various levels of language are often fuzzy indeed.

Form

Each language has its own rules regarding phrase and sentence formation. In English, Greek, and Hebrew (but not in Aramaic), for example, the definite article must come before the

---

[1]A *predicate* is that part of an utterance that comments on the subject. In Standard English the predicate always consists of at least a verb, but Hebrew and Greek, among other languages, frequently use verbless clauses (subject plus predicate nominative, with what appears to us an ellipsis of the verb *to be;* Gk. *ho anthrōpos kalos,* "the man [is] good"). Strictly speaking, a clause may be coextensive with a full and independent (but simple) sentence. For our purposes, I will restrict the term *clause* to units that are syntactically dependent on other units.

noun to which it is connected: *the man* = *ho anthrōpos* = *ha- 'iš*.
Both English and Greek (but not Hebrew) allow the insertion of
an adjective between the article and the noun: *the good man* = *ho
kalos anthrōpos*. Both Greek and Hebrew (but not English) allow
the adjective, with its own article, to be placed after the noun:
(*the man the good*)² = *ho anthrōpos ho kalos* = *ha- 'iš ha-tob*. And
only Greek allows the insertion of a whole clause between
article and noun: *ho erchomenos eis ton oikon anthrōpos* (*the coming-
into-the-house man* = "the man who is/was coming into the
house").

Both English and Hebrew, having lost most case endings,
rely heavily on a fixed word order to indicate grammatical
relationships among words. Greek, on the other hand, has few
restrictions of that sort. The sentence (a) *The man loved the
woman* is hardly identical in meaning to (b) *The woman loved the
man*. The way we can tell in English who is doing the loving is
precisely by looking at the position of the nouns. But that clue
is completely useless in Greek. Sentence (a) can appear in Greek
in any of these forms:

> *ho anthrōpos ēgapēsen tēn gynaika*
> *ho anthrōpos tēn gynaika ēgapēsen*
> *egapesen ho anthrōpos tēn gynaika*
> *ēgapēsen tēn gynaika ho anthrōpos*
> *tēn gynaika ho anthrōpos ēgapēsen*
> *tēn gynaika ēgapēsen ho anthrōpos*

In order to get the meaning of sentence (b) we simply change
the case of the word for "man" from nominative to accusative
(*ton anthrōpon*), which marks it as the object of the verb, and
"woman" from accusative to nominative (*hē gynē*), which
marks it as the subject. Having done so, we can proceed to use
any of the six patterns above. (Of course, some of these patterns
are more common or likely than the rest, and thus a different
nuance or emphasis can be achieved by choosing one over
another. Note also that the position of the definite article with
respect to its noun is pretty much fixed.)

---

²The asterisk is commonly used to indicate linguistic forms that are unattested
or grammatically unacceptable.

In the course of interpreting a biblical passage, students of Greek and Hebrew often find it necessary to consult standard grammars. Sometimes we merely need to identify an unusual form, and so we turn to the section entitled "Morphology" or "Accidence." More often than not, however, what we are really after is help in figuring out the particular force of a grammatical construction, and for that we must look under "Syntax." Rather than attempt a comprehensive and superficial survey of this field, let us consider in some detail the problems involved in interpreting nominal cases and verbal tenses. By doing so we should find it possible to formulate general principles that will prove applicable to most other syntactical problems.

Meaning: Case Relationships

As noted earlier, Hebrew (and Aramaic) do not make much use of case endings. Other means are available, however, for expressing syntactical relationships involving nouns. In particular, Hebrew makes frequent use of the so-called *construct state*, whereby two nominal forms are brought into close relationship. The resulting meanings are quite varied, and they parallel roughly the nuances conveyed by the cases (such as genitive and dative) in Greek. For example, just as the Greek genitive can be interpreted as subjective or objective, so a similar distinction is possible in Hebrew.[3] In Isaiah 9:7 (Heb. v. 6) we find the phrase *qin'at Yhwh*, "the zeal of the LORD"; in 26:11 there is the similar construction *qin'at-'am*, "the zeal of the people." The context makes clear, however, that the relationship being intended in one is quite different from the other. The

---

[3]That is, the noun in the genitive construction functions as either the subject or the object of an implied verb. The English phrase *the love of God* contains two nouns, *love* and *God*. We could say that *of God* is a genitive construction and that the phrase contains an implied verb, *to love*. If the speaker intends to refer to God's love for us, then the phrase is a subjective genitive, because *God* functions as the subject of the implied verb. If what is in view is our love for God, then it is an objective genitive, because *God* functions as the direct object. The example from Isaiah is taken from A. B. Davidson, *Hebrew Syntax*, 3d ed. (Edinburgh: T. & T. Clark, 1901), p. 31. For a detailed classification scheme and numerous examples, see Waltke and O'Connor, *Biblical Hebrew Syntax* § 9.5.

complete clause in the first passage is translated, "the zeal of the LORD Almighty will accomplish this" (subjective genitive, since the reference is to God's own zeal); in the second passage, more or less literally, "they will see zeal [for] the people" (objective genitive, because the people are the object rather than the source of the zeal; cf. NIV, "let them see your zeal for your people").

One of the first things that students of the biblical languages learn is that Greek has five distinct cases. The vocative case ending, used infrequently to indicate the person being spoken to, is fairly straightforward and does not concern us here. The nominative and the accusative, as we noticed above, are used primarily to indicate the subject and the direct object, and this distinction seldom creates exegetical problems (though certain other uses of the accusative can prove puzzling to the beginning student). Most interpretive questions arise in attempting to identify the precise relationship expressed by the dative[4] and (especially) the genitive.

Heavily influenced by the historical bias of nineteenth-century comparative linguistics, some New Testament scholars have argued, on the basis of the Sanskrit case system, that Greek originally had three other cases: the *ablative*, which had the "basic" idea of origin or separation but merged in form with the genitive; and the *instrumental* and *locative*, both of which merged with the dative. The great American grammarian A. T. Robertson adopted this approach and used it to describe the Greek cases in the New Testament.[5] This historical reconstruc-

---

[4]A frequent and noncontroversial use of the dative is that of indicating the indirect object of the verb. "The woman [subject] gave a book [direct object] to the men [indirect object]" would be expressed, *hē gynē edōke biblion tois anthrōpois* (the *-ois* ending here is the marker for the dative plural).

[5]A. T. Robertson, *A Grammar of the Greek New Testament in the Light of Historical Research*, 4th ed. (Nashville, Tenn.: Broadman, 1934), pp. 446–48. Quoting B. Green, he argued that "in every instance the true method of explanation of any particular idiom is to trace its connection to the general meaning of the original Aryan [= Indo-European] case" (p. 447). Robertson was followed, among many, by H. E. Dana and Julius R. Mantey, who wrote one of the most popular and thus influential intermediate-level textbooks in this country, *A Manual Grammar of the Greek New Testament* (New York: Macmillan, 1957); see especially pp. 65–68.

tion is probably not too far from the truth, but even if it could be fully validated, we would have no good reason to adopt it as the proper framework with which to describe (as opposed to "explain the origins of") the cases in Hellenistic Greek. The very fact that these two extra cases cannot be distinguished from the others by their form tells us something about the speakers' linguistic consciousness. And if someone argues that the distinctive meanings if not the forms of these two cases can still be identified,[6] one must respond that such evidence would also justify creating numerous other "cases" to account for the many different meanings conveyed—such as the "temporal case" when the dative is used to indicate time, or the "caring case" when the genitive is used after such verbs as *epimeleomai* ("take care") and *pronoeomai* ("provide")!

So rule number one for interpreting the cases is to avoid being unduly influenced by historical data drawn from a previous stage of the language. A second important principle has to do with recognizing the close connection that obtains between case endings and prepositions. Both of these linguistic features function very much the same way, and in some respects they are interchangeable. Most of the syntactical relationships expressed with prepositions-plus-case can be expressed by case endings alone. For example, the instrumental idea "with the sword" occurs in Luke 22:49 as *en machairē*, but simply as *machairē* in Acts 12:2. Perhaps because prepositions are less ambiguous than cases (though not by much!), once a language begins to use prepositions, case endings become less important.[7]

---

[6]As Robertson himself states, "There are indeed some instances where either of the blended cases will make sense. . . . But such occasional ambiguity is not surprising and these instances on the 'border-line' made syncretism possible. In general the context makes it perfectly clear which of the syncretistic cases is meant" (*Grammar*, p. 448).

[7]That statement is of course historical in nature. We do have evidence that in its earlier stages Greek used prepositions less frequently; in fact, comparative linguists can demonstrate that prepositions are a "late" development in the history of Greek and other languages. By medieval times, Greek case endings were much more restricted in use than they were in the Hellenistic period. In Modern Greek, all prepositions take the same case.

Prepositions have in fact taken over completely in Modern English and other languages.

It may be helpful for the English student to reflect on the parallels between English prepositions and Greek case endings. It is very difficult to describe the "meaning" of a preposition, since its force depends so heavily on the context. If we were asked, for example, what is the meaning of *with*, we would possibly first think of "association" or "companionship," as in *The American soldier spent time with his friends*. But then we might think of a quite different, almost opposite, idea, "against": *The American soldier fought with the Japanese*. Or we are reminded of "instrument": *The American soldier struck the enemy with his rifle*. Or something close to "responsibility": *The general left the orders with the soldier*. Or "manner": *The soldier discharged his mission with grace*. We can list more than two dozen ideas, some of them quite disparate from the others, that can be expressed with this preposition!

It is interesting that English speakers are only vaguely aware of this wide flexibility. They do not have to be taught in first grade that there is a "with of companionship" and an "instrumental with," etc.; and yet they rarely fail to catch the force of the preposition. Most important, no one tries to explain what a preposition means in a particular sentence by appealing to a different use of that preposition. If we saw the phrase "with grace" and we wanted to analyze it or explain it to a foreign student, it would probably not occur to us to say, "The literal or basic meaning of *with* is 'companionship.'" A comment of that sort would be at best irrelevant and at worst confusing. Yet that is one of the most common ways in which modern writers, including some competent scholars, try to explain the use of case endings.

Labeling syntactical uses (whether of cases or tenses or whatever) is probably a pedagogical necessity: how else can adult students who are not learning Greek as a living language master the syntax? But if they do not get past the labeling, they in fact develop a very artificial understanding of how language works. A related problem is the need to learn the most common or important uses before becoming familiar with the others. For example, a student will be told that the genitive case indicates possession, "of." That is indeed a very common use of the genitive, but then the student assumes that it is the *basic* or *essential* meaning and tries to see it everywhere.

A preacher may come to Mark 11:22, where Jesus says, "Have faith in God." This preacher is serious about his study of the text, so he looks it up in the Greek and finds that the text does not have the preposition "in" and that the word for "God" is in the genitive. Come Sunday morning, the audience will almost certainly hear: "The original says literally, 'Have the faith *of* God,'" followed by various inferences (perhaps theologically sound, perhaps not) that have little or nothing to do with the text at hand. The Greek phrase is of course one instance of what we label the objective genitive: the word in the genitive ("God") acts as the object of the implied verb ("believe"). Because to English ears it sounds very strange to express that idea with the preposition "of," we tend to reject the idea or modify it. One suspects, in fact, that this problem has played a role in the opinion, adopted by some recent interpreters, that the expression *pistis Iēsou Christou* ("faith in Jesus Christ," in Gal. 2:16 et al.) should be translated "the faith [or faithfulness] of Jesus Christ."[8]

But how *can* we know whether the use is objective or something else? Essentially, by the way we determine the meaning of the preposition *with* in English: by means of the

[8]Richard B. Hays, for example, thinks that the objective genitive interpretation does not sound natural. See his important book *The Faith of Jesus Christ: An Investigation of the Narrative Substructure of Galatians 3:1–4:11* (SBLDS 56; Chico, Calif.: Scholars Press, 1983), p. 187. Interesting, but rather fanciful, I think, is William L. Lane's suggestion that Mark 11:22 is not an exhortation but an encouraging statement, "you have the faithfulness of God" (*The Gospel According to Mark* [NICNT; Grand Rapid: Eerdmans, 1974], p. 409). Robertson (*Grammar*, p. 500) recognizes that here is an objective genitive, but misled by his historical approach, confusingly appeals "to the root-idea of the genitive as the case of genus or kind," and interprets this phrase as "the God kind of faith." C. E. B. Cranfield is closer to the truth when he says, "The suggestion that the genitive is subjective—'have the sort of faith God has'—is surely a monstrosity of exegesis" (*The Gospel According to Mark: An Introduction and Commentary* [CGTC; Cambridge: Cambridge University Press, 1974], p. 361).

context. We could point out that neither in Mark 11:22 nor in the broad context of the book does the author seem concerned about our having God's own faith as opposed to someone else's. Indeed, nowhere in the New Testament do we find even one *unambiguous* reference to our having the faith that belongs to God, whereas we come across scores of clear passages that speak about having faith *in* God or Christ.[9] For indisputable instances of *pistis* with the objective genitive, we may refer to Acts 3:16, "faith in his name" (*pistei tou onomatos autou*), and Colossians 2:12, "faith in the power of God" (*pisteōs tēs energeias tou theou*). One wonders if doubts about the objective interpretation of *pistis Iēsou Christou* could have occurred only to a modern Western speaker who had identified the Greek genitive with the meaning "of." At least, I am not aware of any ancient Greek father who even raised the possibility of understanding it as subjective.

We should note, incidentally, that the methods of transformational grammar shed some light on the expression *pistis Iēsou Christou*. One way of describing the ambiguity inherent in such a genitive is to say that it can be interpreted as the grammatical transformation of two different "kernel" constructions, (1) *Iēsous pistei*, "Jesus believes" (possibly *Iēsous pistos estin*, "Jesus is faithful"), and (2) *pisteuein eis Iēsoun*, "to believe in Jesus." Now while the second construction is found several times in Paul (and the concept behind it is central to the New Testament), the first one, in either form, is absent.[10] This kind

---

[9] It may be useful to note that the objective genitive is especially common "with substantives denoting a frame of mind or an emotion." See Herbert Weir Smyth, *Greek Grammar* (Cambridge, Mass.: Harvard University Press, 1956) §1331.

[10] In response to my oral comments on this point, Richard Hays some years ago appealed to 2 Thessalonians 3:13; 2 Timothy 2:13; and 2 Corinthians 4:13. See *Conflict and Context: Hermeneutics in the Americas*, ed. M. L. Branson and C. R. Padilla (Grand Rapids: Eerdmans, 1986), pp. 276–77. No one doubts that the *concept* of Jesus' faithfulness (or even of his believing) is biblical and Pauline; my argument is based on the specific form of Paul's language. But even if those three passages used the name *Jesus*, one would still have to consider the preponderance of the evidence, especially in those contexts (Romans and Galatians) where the debate focuses.

of data is very much part of the context for the construction and should be seen as decisive for our problem.

Note, however, that our use of precise syntactical labels tends to obscure what really goes on when we speak or write. In an unpublished paper, Vern S. Poythress has clearly illustrated this issue.

> Suppose in the course of a conversation I say, "The destruction of the army appalled the political leaders." Many times my audience will automatically pick the proper sense of the "of" construction by means of context. It will never occur to them that the sentence in *isolation* is formally ambiguous.
>
> But suppose someone else overhears just this part of the conversation, and is left in the dark about its meaning. He says to me, "Do you mean that the army destroyed something else or that it was itself destroyed in a battle?" How do I answer? Do I remember the decision I made about the use of the "of" construction at the time I used it? No, I do not. It is impossible to remember a decision that I did not make, but that was, as it were, "made for me" in the act of speaking. What I do, typically, is to recall what I was speaking about, what topic I was discussing. And I report to my interlocutor the facts about that topic, namely that the army was the destroyer (or alternatively the destroyed). My intention was *not* to "choose" a particular force of "of" from among a list of possibilities, but to communicate a certain truth concerning what happened to the army.[11]

Finally, the interpreter must be sensitive to the possibility that a biblical author, when using ambiguous syntax, has in fact produced a "vague" expression. Unfortunately, the concept of vagueness, like that of redundancy,[12] carries a negative association for most people. We must carefully distinguish between, on the one hand, vagueness in the sense of sloppiness (that is, in contexts where some precision is appropriate and expected) and, on the other, vagueness that contributes to effective communication (that is, in contexts where greater precision

[11]Vern S. Poythress, "Is Exegesis Possible? I. A Relational Perspective on Meaning" (unpublished typescript), p. 11.

[12]See above, chap. 3, p. 56.

may mislead the reader or hearer to draw an invalid inference). The term *Siamese* is more precise than *cat*, yet there are many times when we do not wish to call attention to the specific kind of cat we happen to own but rather we simply wish to make a general statement that has broader applicability.

The classic example here is *to euangelion tou Christou*, "the gospel of Christ" (e.g., Phil. 1:27). What precisely is the relationship between the two nouns in this phrase? The gospel that belongs to Christ (genitive of possession)? The gospel that comes from Christ (genitive of source)? The gospel that Christ proclaimed (subjective genitive)? The gospel that proclaims Christ (objective genitive)? Perhaps the very asking of the question throws us off track. Countless readers of Paul's letters, without asking the question, have understood the apostle perfectly well. It would not be quite right to say that Paul meant *all* of these things at once—a suggestion that aims at stressing the richness of the apostle's idiom, but at the expense of misunderstanding the way that language normally works.[13] The point is that Paul was not thinking about any one of these possibilities in particular: he was using a general ("vague") expression that served simply to identify his message.

There is a fine line, however, between recognizing genuine linguistic ambiguity and becoming slipshod in our exegesis. For one thing, we may read a passage that comes across as ambiguous in English, but a careful look shows that the same ambiguity does not exist in the original. In an English translation of a Spanish document, the word *corner* may occur without clear indication whether the writer has in mind, say, the inside of a room or the outside of a building; the original cannot contain such an ambiguity, however, for Spanish uses *rincón* for the former and *esquina* for the latter.[14] Conversely, we

---

[13]Nigel Turner, I think, makes this mistake when he argues that "with a mind like St. Paul's, quicker than his own pen or a scribe's, it will not be unreasonable to distill every ounce of richness from the simple genitives of abstract qualities which abound in his epistles." See his work, *Grammatical Insights into the New Testament* (Edinburgh: T. & T. Clark, 1965), p. 111, and my comments in *Biblical Words*, pp. 150–51.

[14]"Isn't Spanish wonderfully precise?"

could make the mistake of attributing precision to the original where it does not exist, as when Spanish uses *techo* for both "ceiling" and "roof."[15]

But even apart from that consideration, we need to remember that speakers and writers normally have a single meaning in view. In other words, we cannot allow the fact of linguistic vagueness to become an excuse for laziness in grammatical analysis or a pretense for uncontrolled interpretation. Take Galatians 1:12, where Paul insists that the gospel he preaches is not a human product but that it came to him *di' apokalypseōs Iēsou Christou*. Should we take "Jesus Christ" as a subjective genitive (more specifically, of origin) and translate with the NIV, "I received it by revelation from Jesus Christ"? Or should we interpret it as an objective genitive, with the implication, "I received it when God revealed Jesus Christ to me"?

A strong argument in favor of the second interpretation is the fact that only two (Greek) sentences later, Paul uses what could be viewed as the unambiguous kernel clause: God was pleased "to reveal his Son in me" (*apokalypsai ton huion autou en emoi*, v. 16). On the other hand, the first interpretation is supported by the thrust of verse 12 itself, particularly since the phrase in question serves as the direct opposite of "from man" (*para anthrōpou*). Faced by this dilemma, the interpreter will be tempted to avoid a decision by arguing that it must be both, since the two aspects cannot be separated.

What may be conceptually or theologically true, however, is quite a different question from what a linguistic expression actually conveys. It would, I think, be legitimate to say, "We cannot reach a definitive decision on this problem, but the ambiguity does not affect significantly our understanding of Paul's point, since the two ideas are closely related and both are reflected in this very passage." On the other hand, it is probably misleading to argue that Paul intended to communicate these

---

[15]"Can't Spanish speakers tell the difference between an interior and an exterior surface?!"

two distinct ideas with the one expression *di' apokalypseōs Iēsou Christou*.

At any rate, we can probably reach a decision. The other two Pauline uses of this construction (1 Cor. 1:7; 2 Thess. 1:7; both referring to the Second Coming) are unambiguously objective. Moreover, the objective interpretation does not at all contradict or even minimize Paul's emphasis on the origin of his gospel: given the fact that he received the gospel on the occasion when Jesus Christ was manifested to him, the message he preaches cannot possibly be attributed to human invention.

Meaning: Tense and Aspect

Perhaps no feature of the biblical languages is the source of more confusion and fanciful interpretation than the verbal "tenses." Beginning Greek students, upon being confronted with the term *aorist* (which is normally not used in English grammar), tend to inject quasi-mysterious associations into it. After all, they are first taught that it is roughly equivalent to the simple past tense (preterite) in English, only to find out, a few weeks later, that the Greek imperative can have an aorist as well as a present form. How can one request a person today to do something yesterday? And when the teacher informs the students that the aorist does not really indicate time, they become ripe either for experiencing total bewilderment or for developing preposterous exegesis.

And things hardly get better when they move into Hebrew class. Fairly early on they are told that Hebrew has only two tenses, "perfect" and "imperfect," as though the Israelites were unable to talk about the present and the future. And sooner or later the class is granted the ultimate oracle: merely add the Hebrew word for "and" to the verb, and lo, the perfect becomes imperfect and the imperfect becomes perfect! Fortunately or unfortunately (depending on one's point of view), this revelation is too much for most seminarians, who tend to ignore what little Hebrew they learned and return to the more fertile ground of Greek grammar.

Surely the first step out of this mire is to appreciate that there is nothing peculiar about verbs that indicate *aspect* (= how is the action presented by the speaker) rather than *time* (= when does the action take place).[16] In English, for example, the difference between *John wrote a letter* and *John was writing a letter* is not one of temporal reference: both verbal constructions could be used when referring to the *one* event that took place, say, last Monday evening. Rather, the distinction is an aspectual one: the second expression indicates progressive action (to use a traditional category), while the first one does not. Moreover, English has the lexical means to express a wide variety of aspectual distinctions: *used to write; kept on writing; started to write*.

There are indeed some differences between English and the biblical languages, and it is those differences that create confusion. Whereas English verbs, whatever else they do, always seem to indicate time reference,[17] a rather large number of languages around the world manage quite nicely, thank you, with verbs that do not by themselves have that reference. The

[16]Strictly speaking, verbal aspect too has something to do with time, and so it would be more accurate to distinguish between *aspectual time* and *deictic time*. See John Lyons, *Semantics*, 2 vols. (Cambridge: Cambridge University Press, 1977), vol. 2, chap. 15, especially pp. 677–90; and Bernard Comrie, *Aspect: An Introduction to the Study of Verbal Aspect and Related Problems* (CTL, Cambridge: Cambridge University Press, 1976), especially pp. 1–6. For more technical and wide-ranging discussions, see Östen Dahl, *Tense and Aspect Systems* (Oxford: Blackwell, 1985), and the anthology edited by Paul J. Hopper, *Tense-Aspect: Between Semantics and Pragmatics, Containing the Contributions to a Symposium on Tense and Aspect, Held at UCLA, May 1979* (Typological Studies in Language 1; Amsterdam/Philadelphia: John Benjamins, 1982). Special note must be taken of Juan Mateos, *El aspecto verbal en el Nuevo Testamento* (Estudios de Nuevo Testamento 1; Madrid: Ediciones Cristiandad, 1977); Stanley E. Porter, *Verbal Aspect in the Greek of the New Testament: With Special Reference to Tense and Mood* (Studies in Biblical Greek 1; New York: P. Lang, 1989); and B. M. Fanning, *Verbal Aspect in New Testament Greek* (Oxford University Press, 1990). Alviero Niccacci, *The Syntax of the Verb in Classical Hebrew Prose* (JSOTSS 86; Sheffield: JSOT, 1990), makes much use of "text linguistics."

[17]I say "seem" because even in English the temporal element can be obscured. When we say that the earth *moves* around the sun, we are using what some would call a "gnomic present": the point is that the earth is so moving, not only right now, but always—past, present, and future. It has even been suggested that the English present is best described as a "nonpast."

speakers of these languages, of course, can indicate the time through lexical and other means (*yesterday, tomorrow,* the context of the utterance, etc.), but the verbal form itself gives no hint. Greek does grammaticalize temporal reference by, for example, adding the prefix *e-* (called an *augment*) to indicate past tense: the verb *krinomen,* "we judge," can become *ekrinomen,* "we were judging," or *ekrinamen,* "we judged."

In biblical Hebrew, however, the situation is different, since the two tenses mentioned above do not necessarily indicate past-present-future. That is why English translations (particularly in the poetic sections, where the context gives no explicit indication of time) vary significantly in their rendering of the tenses, as in Psalm 27:2:

> When the wicked, *even* mine enemies and my foes, came upon me to eat up my flesh, they stumbled and fell. (KJV)

> When evildoers close in on me to devour me,
>   it is my enemies, my assailants,
>   who stumble and fall. (NEB)

> When evil men advance against me
>   to devour my flesh,
> when my enemies and my foes attack me,
>   they will stumble and fall. (NIV)

The two main verbs in the sentence ("stumble" and "fall"—the two other verbs are infinitives) occur here in the so-called perfect tense. Because the character of the English verbal system forces the translator to indicate the temporal reference, which is nonexistent in the Hebrew, KJV translated the verbs as past, NEB as present, NIV as future. Note that in this context the tense does not alter the message of the psalmist. A translation in the past does not exclude a reference to the present or future; on the contrary, the past event would be the basis for later confidence. A translation in the future, on the other hand, could well reflect the psalmist's *previous* experience. The point, however, is that the psalmist has not explicitly indicated a time reference: the Hebrew verbal system allows him to "get away with" this ambiguity without jeopardizing (indeed, perhaps it enhances) the central message that God always protects his people.[18]

Another important difference between English and the biblical languages is that English depends heavily on the vocabulary to indicate aspect; that is, aspectual distinctions are seldom grammaticalized. Even the distinction between *John wrote* and *John was writing*, since it involves a periphrasis (adding the helping verb *was* to form the imperfect), is regarded by some linguists as more lexical than grammatical. A clearer example, already noted, is *used to write*, an idea a Greek writer can express grammatically, by using the imperfect tense. Consider also the verbs *obtain* and *have*: the former verb can be understood as expressing the incipient or ingressive aspect of an action involving "possession," while the latter verb expresses a resultative or stative aspect of the same action. Greek can achieve the same goal by merely alternating the tenses of the same verb.[19]

These differences, though important, must not obscure what is more *fundamentally common* between English and the biblical languages. The primary consideration here is that aspectual choices are usually unconscious and to a large extent dictated either by the requirements of the grammar or by the thrust of the context. Very rarely, if ever, does an English speaker or writer pause to consider whether a simple past tense or an imperfect should be used: the decision is virtually automatic. When the decision is not an obvious one, English speakers would have some difficulty distinguishing between the two. Note these two questions: (1) *How do you feel today?* (2) *How are you feeling today?* What exactly is the difference

---

[18]For a very valuable survey of the debate concerning the Hebrew conjugations, see Waltke and O'Connor, *Biblical Hebrew Syntax*, chap. 29.

[19]For example, in Romans 1:13 Paul expresses his desire to "have" (*schō*, aorist subjunctive of *echō*); the nuance is clearly "to start having," "to receive." In this case, English "have" adequately conveys that idea. Notice, however, Philem. 7: "Your love has given me great joy and encouragement" (NIV). A literal translation would be, "I had [*eschen*, aorist indicative = I received, obtained] much joy and encouragement because of your love." See also J. H. Moulton, *Grammar of New Testament Greek*, vol. 1 (3d ed.; Edinburgh: T. & T. Clark, 1908), pp. 110, 145.

between these utterances? Even specialists in English grammar cannot agree. And we would certainly get nowhere if we asked a particular speaker what made him or her choose one of these questions over the other! We would go too far if we were to argue that a writer's decision between, say, an aorist and a present subjunctive never reflects a stylistic decision that may be of some interest to the interpreter. But we can feel confident that no reasonable writer would seek to express a major point by leaning on a subtle grammatical distinction—especially if it is a point not otherwise clear from the whole context (and if it *is* clear from the context, then the grammatical subtlety plays at best a secondary role in exegesis).

A second consideration in interpreting tenses is that the usual labels can prove misleading. Grammar books of New Testament Greek, for example, often use the terms *linear* and *punctiliar* to express the force of the present (or imperfect) and the aorist respectively. If very carefully defined and qualified, these labels might be of some value, but we would be much better off getting rid of them. When ancient Greek grammarians coined the term *aorist* (from *horizō*, "determine, define," plus the privative or negating alpha), they correctly perceived that this tense was "undetermined," that is, general or even vague, exactly the opposite of what most Greek students, and not a few professional exegetes, think. The aorist was normally used to refer to an action as a whole, a complete event; thus it was the tense chosen when the writer did *not* want to say something special about the action. The label *punctiliar*, however, suggests to students a momentary event (contrast Rev. 20:4, the martyrs "reigned [*ebasileusan*, aor. ind.] with Christ a thousand years"!), and that in turn leads people to think of emphasis, definitiveness, once-for-allness, and other related ideas not at all inherent in the aorist.[20] How misguided is the popular notion that the aorist can serve to emphasize the once-for-all character of Christ's death (a truth clearly expressed by the whole context of several passages, not by grammatical subtlety) may be

---

[20]For examples, cf. D. A. Carson, *Exegetical Fallacies* (Grand Rapids: Baker, 1984), pp. 69–72.

demonstrated from the author of Hebrews, who was certainly a master of the Greek language. In 9:26 he tells us that if Christ were like other priests, he "would have had to suffer many times since the creation of the world." The adverb *pollakis* ("many times, frequently") would seem to require a present tense; in fact, it modifies the verb "suffer," *pathein*, which is the aorist infinitive of *paschō* (Cf. also 2 Cor. 11:24–25).

One final, and important, consideration is that aspectual distinctions reflect the speaker's subjective perspective rather than objective reality. Suppose someone says, *When I examined the building, I was eating my lunch*. We could describe the verb *examined* as aoristic and *was eating* as imperfective; the former views the complete action of "examining" in its totality,[21] while the latter looks "internally" at the ongoing (noncomplete) event of eating. However, one might describe the *same* event as follows: *When I ate my lunch, I was examining the building*. In this case, it is the act of eating that the speaker is looking at, as it were, from the outside, while the act of examining is presented as ongoing. We can therefore see that a speaker or writer can refer to the same objective reality with different aspects, and so the aspectual decision only tells us how he or she is perceiving it and presenting it, not whether the reality is *intrinsically* progressive in character, or punctiliar, or whatever.

Even these qualifications may not be sufficient to discourage exegetes from overinterpreting aspectual distinctions. A

---

[21]That is, "the whole of the situation is presented as a single unanalysable whole, with beginning, middle, and end rolled into one; nc attempt is made to divide this situation up into the various individual phases that make up the action" (Comrie, *Aspect*, p. 3). However, as my colleague Vern S. Poythress has pointed out in personal conversation, the alternation of tenses in a narrative may well be primarily a function of discourse, that is, the need to relate the various actions to one another. If so, even a description of aspects that focuses on the way the speaker or writer *views* the action may turn out to be an overinterpretation. Cf. the introductory chapter in *Tense-Aspect* (ed. Hopper), where the editor proposes to view aspect "as an essentially discourse-level, rather than a semantic, sentence-level phenomenon. . . . My proposal does not, so far as I can see, conflict with the recognized achievements of recent work on aspect, but it does argue that our understanding of aspect should be rooted in the last resort in discourse" (p. 16).

classic example is the difficult statement in 1 John 3:6, which we may translate literally, "Everyone who remains in him does not sin [ouch hamartanei]." Is John setting forth here the doctrine of sinless perfection? A very popular solution to the problem is to focus on the present tense of the verb and argue on that basis that John must have in mind a habitual and unrepentant life of sin. Even the NIV reflects this understanding: "No one who lives in him keeps on sinning." It is perhaps possible to defend such an interpretation of the verse on broad theological grounds, but the argument based on aspectual distinction simply will not work. While Greek has an aorist/imperfect contrast in the past tenses of the indicative, no such contrast exists in the present tense. Since Greek does not have an "aoristic" form in the present tense, John had no choice but to use the present form.[22] The use of hamartanei, in other words, conveys a temporal piece of information (present or gnomic rather than past or future), not an aspectual perspective as such.

But what about the aorist/present distinction in the other moods, such as the imperative and the subjunctive? One often hears that the present imperatives in Matthew 7:7 indicate continuation and perseverance and that therefore we should translate, "Keep on asking and it will be given to you; keep on seeking and you will find; keep on knocking and the door will be opened to you." It is true that one of the functions of the present imperative is to indicate a command or request when the action in view is already in progress, while the aorist is more commonly used when the action has not begun, with the implication "Start doing." However, the distinction does not

---

[22]Of course, John might have used a paraphrastic construction, but that would have contained, if anything, an even stronger "progressive" nuance. In the following clause, John uses a present participle, ho hamartanōn, "the one sinning," which can be contrasted with the aorist form. The function of the aorist participle, however, is to refer to action prior to the action of the main verb. If John had used the aorist participle, the meaning would have been "he who has sinned," so the argument does not work for this clause either. In verse 9 John uses the present infinitive, dynatai hamartanein, which can indeed be contrasted aspectually with the aorist form. Even in moods other than the indicative, however, aspectual distinctions are not normally used to make a substantive point. See further below.

always hold up. When 1 John 5:21 commands, "Guard [aor. *phylaxate*] yourselves from idols," are we to understand, "Start guarding yourselves," as though the recipients of the letter were already guilty of idolatry? Even when the distinction holds, we need to keep in mind that the choice of the aspect is largely determined by the circumstances; that is, the choice is not made in order to accentuate the point.[23] The whole thrust of Matthew 7:7, of course, is the need for persistence in prayer. One is not surprised, therefore, to see the imperatives in the present tense; but it is quite improbable that the verbal form by itself ever conveys the notion of perseverance.

In conclusion, we may say that an interpreter is unwise to emphasize an idea that allegedly comes from the use of a tense (or some other subtle grammatical distinction) unless the context as a whole clearly sets forth that idea. Whether the use of the tense contributes to that idea or whether it is the idea that contributes to the use of the tense is perhaps debatable, but no interpretation is worth considering unless it has strong contextual support. If it doesn't, then the use of the grammatical detail becomes irrelevant; if it does, then the grammar is at best a pointer to, not the basis of, the correct interpretation.

PARAGRAPHS AND LARGER UNITS

Traditionally, grammar books have stopped at the sentence level when describing syntax. The past two decades or so, however, have witnessed a vigorous interest in how sentences are linked with one another to form paragraphs and how paragraphs are put together to construct a whole discourse. The resulting discipline is variously called *text linguistics, discourse grammar, discourse analysis,* etc. Almost by definition, the boundaries of this discipline are rather fuzzy. One can pick up

---

[23]Note that in the Lord's Prayer, Matthew 6:11 has the aorist *dos*, "give," which we may say is grammatically appropriate in the context of the word "today." Luke 11:3, on the other hand, has "every day," and so the form of the verb is present, *didou*. The point is that the idea of repetition or continuation is presented primarily by the explicit "every day," only secondarily and implicitly by the verbal aspect.

several books claiming to deal with discourse and find only partial overlapping among them. One author may view the field primarily as sociological in character, but another one as anthropological or even psychological; one author is interested in conversation and another one in the plot progression of narratives; and so on.[24]

Moreover, the discipline is rather young, characterized by gaps in research and a fluctuating terminology. Indeed, only a few years ago an important textbook acknowledged that "workers in discourse analysis have only a partial understanding of even the most-studied ingredients."[25] Rather than attempt a thorough presentation, therefore, I will only sample some of the concerns of discourse analysts. In spite of the differences among researchers, there is one theme that comes up again and again in

---

[24]Two early works, both comprehensive and influential, are Teun A. Van Dijk, *Some Aspects of Text Grammars: A Study in Theoretical Linguistics and Poetics* (Janua linguarum, ser. mai. 63; The Hague/Paris: Mouton, 1972), and Joseph Grimes, *The Thread of Discourse* (Janua linguarum, ser. min. 207; The Hague/Paris: Mouton, 1975). A good textbook focusing on conversation is Malcolm Coulthard, *An Introduction to Discourse Analysis* (Applied Linguistics and Language Study; London: Longman, 1977). Wholly devoted to formulating the criteria that determine "textuality" (that is, whether a string of utterances constitutes a unified text) is Robert de Beaugrande and Wolfgang Dressler, *Introduction to Text Linguistics* (Longman Linguistics Library 26; London: Longman, 1981). I have profited greatly from the comprehensive survey by Enrique Bernárdez, *Introducción a la lingüística del texto* (Madrid: Espasa-Calpe, 1982). The sociological approach is well represented by Michael Stubbs, *Discourse Analysis: The Sociolinguistic Analysis of Natural Language* (Language in Society 4; Chicago: University of Chicago Press, 1983). An emphasis on narrative, arising out of much anthropological experience, characterizes the work of Robert E. Longacre, *The Grammar of Discourse* (New York and London: Plenum, 1983). For a strictly linguistic perspective, see especially Gillian Brown and George Yule, *Discourse Analysis* (Cambridge Textbooks in Linguistics; Cambridge: Cambridge University Press, 1983). One may gauge recent advances in this field through the anthologies (often quite technical) published in the series Research in Text Theory / Untersuchungen zur Texttheorie, under the general editorship of János S. Petöfi. Among the latest in this series is number 11, *Literary Discourse: Aspects of Cognitive and Social Psychological Approaches*, ed. L. Halász (Berlin/New York: Walter de Gruyter, 1987).

[25]Brown and Yule, *Discourse Analysis*, p. 270.

the literature, and that is the desire to understand *what language is used for*. This "functional" or "pragmatic" approach reflects a dissatisfaction with the tendency, even in "modern" linguistics, to examine sentences more or less in isolation, that is, by deliberately removing them from the speaker's or writer's purpose in uttering those sentences. In the field(s) of discourse analysis, therefore, no concept is more crucial than that of *context*.

Form

What formal means do languages have to mark the various possible relationships among sentences? Consider the following examples:

> Mary fell. She broke her wrist.
> Mary fell and [she] broke her wrist.
> Mary broke her wrist because she fell.

These are only three out of the many different ways in which English can express the connection between the two concepts, "Mary fell" and "Mary broke her wrist." In the first example there appears to be no connector, but in fact the pronoun *she*, referring back to the subject of the previous sentence, serves effectively to link the two sentences. In the second example, the two ideas are formally but vaguely connected by means of the coordinating conjunction *and*, which by itself does not make explicit the nature of the connection. In the last example, the sentence relationship is made clearer with the subordinating conjunction *because*.

All three of these techniques are also used in the biblical languages, but even a beginning student will quickly notice a difference in frequency. Hebrew narrative, for example, is characterized by an almost endless string of *and*s. Greek story-tellers, insofar as they use conjunctions, alternate between *kai* ("and") and *de* ("but," "now"); in addition, however, they will often use such adverbs as *euthys* (characteristic of Mark), *tote* ("then," characteristic of Matthew), *oun* ("therefore"), etc. Most striking of all is the frequency with which Greek writers use participles to link clauses (rather than "independent" sentences) together. The technique is certainly available in English: *Falling down, Mary broke her wrist* (the closest that Hebrew can come to this adverbial use of the participle is by using the so-called infinitive absolute). Nevertheless, the abundance of adverbial participles, as well as their flexibility, is one of the truly distinctive features of Ancient Greek.

In addition to linking one clause (or sentence) to the next one, speakers have ways of indicating that a series of sentences belong together as part of a larger unit, which we may call the *paragraph.* Defining linguistic units is never easy—scholars have vigorously disagreed even over the proper way of determining what constitutes a word! The debate becomes much more complicated when they seek to define a paragraph.[26] Of course, we do not have in mind here an "orthographic" paragraph, that is, a chunk of text that begins with an indented line. Such a printing technique may indeed mark a shift in topic, but not always: the audience in view, for example, or even the width of the column, may dictate breaking up the text into smaller pieces.

Sometimes we are very explicit in marking a shift: *Let's move on to a related topic,* or, *To change the subject . . . .* At other times the shift is less obvious but still formally marked by such expressions as *Now, Moreover,* and *On the other hand.* Just as frequently, especially in informal conversation, we dispense with any formal markers because it is fairly obvious, from the tone or the general context, that there is some disjunction between the last string of utterances and the string that is about to begin. All of these conditions can be found in the biblical languages. A Hebrew narrative will often mark the beginning of a paragraph with *wayhi* ("And it was," reflected sometimes in the New Testament with *kai egeneto*); Paul may introduce a new section in his letters with *gnōrizō de hymin* ("Now I make known to you") or a similar clause. More sophisticated techniques can also be used, such as *inclusio,* whereby a

---

[26]Cf. ibid., pp. 95–100.

paragraph is explicitly bracketed, that is, it begins and ends with the same or similar word(s).[27]

Not infrequently, however, formal markers are absent, and we need to depend on other features to identify the paragraph boundaries. Careful students of literary texts, long before the development of discourse analysis, have appreciated the exegetical value of noticing such boundaries (usually reflected in a commentator's outline, for example). Modern linguistics cannot replace the "common sense" skills of a good interpreter—indeed, it has the potential for an exaggerated formalism that can swallow up those skills—but it can provide new perspectives and methods leading to greater consistency.

Although I need not here catalog all the formal features that contribute to the unity of a paragraph, I must mention a technique that has received increasing attention among biblical scholars. It has long been noticed that short portions of discourse (even modern conversations) sometimes take the form, A-B-B'-A', known as *chiasm*. Note Galatians 4:4–5:

A   God sent his Son,
   B   born of a woman, born under law,
   B'   to redeem those under law,
A'   that we might receive the full right of sons.[28]

Lines A and A' parallel each other (we could say they form an *inclusio*), and so do B and B'. The pattern is very common in

---

[27]It has been suggested, for example, that the noun *prokopē*, "advance," in Philippians 1:12 and 25 (otherwise found only once in the New Testament: 1 Tim. 4:15) formally marks the unit that extends from verse 12 to verse 26 (vv. 25–26 constitute one sentence). For a detailed attempt to identify paragraph breaks in the epistles of Paul, see John R. Werner, "Discourse Analysis of the Greek New Testament," in *The New Testament Student and His Field* (The NT Student 5, ed. J. H. Skilton [Phillipsburg, N.J.: Presbyterian and Reformed, 1982]), pp. 213–33, which includes an analysis of 2 Thessalonians originally prepared by Robert H. Sterner.

[28]This common example was noted over a century ago by J. B. Lightfoot, *The Epistle to the Galatians* (London: Macmillan, 1865), p. 168. It is very probable that Philippians 1:15–17 was written by Paul in a chiastic form, as attested by all early manuscripts. Later copyists, however, transposed verses 16 and 17 so as to produce a more common parallel structure (A-B-A'-B', with negative motives mentioned in verse 15a and verse 16, positive in verse 15b and verse 17). This latter form, found in a majority of (late) manuscripts, is reflected in the KJV. Cf. my comments in *Philippians*, p. 74.

Hebrew poetry and has been clearly detected in larger units, not only consisting of a large paragraph but even containing many paragraphs within it.

Among many interesting examples, we may note the proposal that a large chiastic structure characterizes a major section of 2 Chronicles:

A   Solomon's wealth and wisdom (1:1–17)
   B   Recognition by Gentiles / dealings with Hiram (2:1–16)
      C   Temple construction / gentile labor (2:17–5:1)
         D   Dedication of temple (5:2–7:10)
         D'   Divine response (7:11–22)
      C'   Other construction / gentile labor (8:1–16)
   B'   Recognition by Gentiles / dealings with Hiram (8:17–9:12)
A'   Solomon's wealth and wisdom (9:13–28).[29]

At times this approach gets out of hand, as when John Bligh "discovers" that the whole Epistle to the Galatians is one large chiasm, composed of many subchiasms and sub-sub-chiasms.[30] More often than not, proposals of this sort are characterized by acknowledged irregularities, textual emendations, and source-critical surgery. It would be a mistake, however, to deny the presence of chiastic structure in many biblical passages or to ignore its value for exegesis.

Meaning

What was Paul trying to do when he used a particular conjunction or when he grouped together a specific string of sentences? Another way of phrasing the question is quite simply, What did Paul mean? The functional concern that characterizes discourse analysis is therefore inseparable from

---

[29]Adapted from Raymond B. Dillard, 2 Chronicles (WBC 15; Waco: Word, 1987), pp. 5–6.

[30]John Bligh, Galatians in Greek: A Structural Analysis of St. Paul's Epistle to the Galatians, with Notes on the Greek (Detroit: University of Detroit Press, 1966). Cf. also Kenneth Bailey, Poet and Peasant: A Literary Cultural Approach to the Parables in Luke (Grand Rapids: Eerdmans, 1976), pp. 79–85, and my review in WTJ 41 (1978–79): 213–15.

semantics. The inverse is also true: semantics is inseparable from discourse—meaning cannot be discovered apart from context. At the beginning of this chapter I noted that only occasionally can a word by itself be used to convey meaning. Normally, meaning is conveyed by whole propositions. But now we must go a step further and recognize that we do not normally convey meaning by single propositions, but by propositions that form part of a larger whole (including the situation common to speaker and hearer).

We can certainly think of partial exceptions. *Give me liberty or give me death!* is an isolated sentence that communicates a great deal of meaning, but even here we fool ourselves if we do not recognize that there is much prior information (historical knowledge, national identification, familiarity with the statement itself, etc.) that makes the utterance so meaningful. All of that information constitutes the context that provides the necessary semantic framework. The best biblical examples of propositions that seem to convey meaning in isolation are the pithy sayings in the Book of Proverbs. Yet how easy it is for readers to misuse those sayings, converting them into comfortable moralistic principles that sit quite well with pagan presuppositions. In the context of the book as a whole, with its emphasis on true wisdom as the fear of the Lord—to say nothing of the biblical and redemptive context more generally—the meaning may be quite different.

More to the point, we should note that even the smallest books of the Bible consist of whole discourses. If propositions by themselves were quite sufficient, the Scriptures might be composed of a long list of individual sayings. Instead, God has given us narratives (some quite long), hymns, letters. And these various portions are brought together in a coherent and unified whole. The principle that the Bible is its own best interpreter is not wishful thinking.[31] From one perspective, this principle is but a reflection of the nature of all communication: sentences

---

[31]See vol. 1 of this Foundations of Contemporary Interpretation series, *Has the Church Misread the Bible? The History of Interpretation in the Light of Current Issues* (Grand Rapids: Zondervan, 1987), pp. 92–94.

must be understood in the light of their total context. Even if we are reading Plato, we cannot artificially wrench one proposition in the *Republic* from the philosopher's whole thought. From another perspective, however, this principle is unique to Scripture. For those who are persuaded that the Bible comes from God in a sense that is not true of other writings, its unity and coherence take on a completely new dimension. God does not fail to speak in a consistent fashion—as Plato or an uninspired Paul might—and thus individual propositions in Scripture do perfectly cohere with other propositions and shed light on each other.

In our effort to interpret the Bible, therefore, we should give special attention to the way sentences are joined, how they form paragraphs, and how the paragraphs combine to constitute larger units. At the simplest level, this means that we should read the Bible the way we read other literature. When we receive a letter from a friend, do we read the middle paragraph today, the last sentence next week, the introductory section two months from now? Unfortunately, many Christians use precisely that "method" in their reading of Paul's letters. The biblical books were meant to be read as wholes and that is the way we should read them.

At a more specialized level, we should make the effort to identify in some detail textual features connecting propositions to one another and to understand how those features actually function. Even this step is to a large extent accessible to the common believer. Does this sentence give the reason for the preceding one or does it merely expand on it? Does that paragraph build on the previous argument or does it move to a new topic altogether? One can come up with more than two dozen ways of expressing the linkage between any one pair of sentences.[32]

---

[32]Building on the work of such scholars as John Beekman and Robert E. Longacre, and without having to appeal to Hebrew grammar, Vern S. Poythress has illustrated this approach by applying a detailed taxonomy to Isaiah 51:9–11. See his article "Propositional Relations" in *The New Testament Student and His Field* (see above, note 25), pp. 159–212. Cf. also Cotterell and Turner, *Linguistics*, chap. 6. For an impressive and technical application, see

Students of Greek and Hebrew, however, can delve into these questions at greater depth and with greater profit, since English translations are often unable to represent the formal structure of sentences in the original text. Probably the most efficient method is to attempt a visual representation of the syntax, that is, to diagram the clauses and sentences making up a paragraph. One need not learn or develop a complicated method. Merely by indenting the appropriate clauses and labeling them, the student can gain a new appreciation for the flow of the argument.[33]

Consider Romans 1:16–18, first in the NIV rendering:

> I am not ashamed of the gospel, because it is the power of God for the salvation of everyone who believes: first for the Jew, then for the Gentile. For in the gospel a righteousness from God is revealed, a righteousness that is by faith from first to last, just as it is written: "The righteous will live by faith."
>
> The wrath of God is being revealed from heaven against all the godlessness and wickedness of men who suppress the truth by their wickedness. . . .

Now compare a literal rendering (that is, one that tries to represent the formal features of the Greek), accompanied by clearer visual distinctions and some tentative (interpretive) labels:

> For I am not ashamed of the gospel [*response* to anticipated question]
>> for it is the power of God [*reason* for not being ashamed]
>>> unto salvation [*result* of God's power]
>>>> to everyone who believes [*recipients* of salvation]
>>>>> to the Jew first [*expands* on recipients: priority]
>>>>> and to the Greek [*expands* on recipients: universality]
>> for the righteousness of God is revealed in it [*explanation*]
>>> out of faith to faith [*character* of revelation]

Robert E. Longacre, *Joseph: A Story of Divine Providence: A Text Theoretical and Textlinguistic Analysis of Genesis 37 and 39–48* (Winona Lake: Eisenbrauns, 1989).

[33]Very helpful in this connection is the set of guidelines put together by Gordon D. Fee, *New Testament Exegesis: A Handbook for Students and Pastors* (Philadelphia: Westminster, 1983), pp. 60–77.

    as it is written . . . [*proof*]
For the wrath of God is revealed . . . [*contrast*: new paragraph]

If the time and effort often invested in isolated word studies were redirected toward this kind of analysis, Bible students would gain a proportionately greater understanding of what the text says. This approach forces us to ask questions that might otherwise not occur to us—and when we fail to ask these questions, we are left with only a vague impression of how the biblical author is linking together the various parts of his argument or narrative. It should be clear from Romans 1:16–18, for example, that the Greek conjunction *gar* does not always introduce a simple cause for what precedes. Paul uses it to serve a variety of transitional functions that cannot be discovered if we think only about "grammar." We can, in addition, proceed to analyze a portion of text by means of more detailed and sophisticated techniques and terminology.[34] To be sure, one always runs the risk of imposing on the text complicated connections that the biblical author conceived of in only a general way (recall the discussion of the genitive case earlier in this chapter). Nevertheless, students of the Bible tend to make the opposite mistake and pay less attention than they should to the need for determining clause relationships and paragraph units.

Finally, interpreters must give full consideration to the broader context of the passages they analyze. For example, the type of literature (i.e., its genre) can significantly affect the total meaning of a statement. Another volume in the present series has devoted attention to this matter and so we need not pursue it here.[35] Also the occasion and general purpose of a writing can become an important (sometimes definitive) clue. Even a form

---

[34]For an application of this method to a very elegant NT passage, see David Alan Black, "Hebrews 1:1–4: A Study in Discourse Analysis," *WTJ* 49 (1987): 175–94. A fine introduction, with helpful diagrams, is the last chapter of J. P. Louw, *Semantics of New Testament Greek* (SBLSS; Philadelphia: Fortress, and Chico, Calif.: Scholars Press, 1982).

[35]See Tremper Longman III, *Literary Approaches to Biblical Interpretation*, Foundations of Contemporary Interpretation 3 (Grand Rapids: Zondervan, 1988), especially pp. 73–83.

of address, such as *Mr. Smith*, can "mean" something positive (a courteous touch in a business letter) or something quite negative (a reproachful tone when writing to a close acquaintance). Whether Paul intended his letter to the Romans as a theological treatise more or less abstracted from historical circumstances or as a "real" letter directly provoked by those historical circumstances will substantially affect our interpretation. In the first instance, chapters 9–11 (to take but one example) may be, and often have been, perceived as something of a parenthesis; alternatively, if the letter was motivated by the struggles arising out of the Judaistic controversy, those chapters take on a much more prominent role, possibly the crowning argument in a whole series of answers to objections that had been raised against Paul's gospel.

7

EPILOGUE—PASSING IT ON

Throughout this small book we have treated our subject as though we had immediate access to it, as though nothing whatever could come between us and the biblical text. It is true that at the most fundamental level Christians enjoy direct access to God and that his Spirit directly witnesses to our spirit through the Scriptures. On the other hand, we cannot allow this precious truth to degenerate into a sense of personal infallibility. For one thing, our own finitude and sinfulness get in the way of perfect understanding.[1] Then again, we are greatly removed in time and culture from the writings that make up the Bible.

But there is an additional matter that needs to be considered, if only in summary fashion, and that is the process of *transmission*. In one sense we have been dealing with this matter all along, insofar as communication—and therefore the transmission of information, emotions, etc.—is inherent to language itself. It may prove helpful, nevertheless, to discuss briefly some other important aspects of linguistic transmission.

---

[1] I have discussed this important issue in *Has the Church Misread the Bible?* (see esp. pp. 86–89).

129

TEXTUAL TRANSMISSION

Every time a scribe sat down to copy one or several of the books of the Bible he became involved in the process of transmitting the text, and therefore the language, of the Scriptures. Of course, we have no direct access to the original manuscripts used by Luke or Paul, but only to such later copies as were produced by scribes. We must recognize that this process creates a certain distance between us and the text. And just as we do what we can to bridge, for example, the *cultural* distance that separates us from the Bible by learning about archaeology, so also we must make every effort to bridge the *textual* distance, that is, to remove from the text alien elements introduced by scribes. In short, we must be prepared to do textual criticism.

All literary works go through comparable processes of transmission. Many important works from the ancient world have not survived at all, while most of those that have survived are represented by very few and often fragmented manuscripts. In contrast, manuscripts of the New Testament (in whole or in part) are very numerous, easily exceeding—both in numbers and in antiquity—the most famous classical works.[2] With regard to the Old Testament books, the numbers are not as great, but two important factors compensate for that: (1) the primary tradition, known as the Masoretic Text and reaching back into Late Antiquity (though extant manuscripts were produced during the Middle Ages), is characterized by exceptional homogeneity and accuracy; (2) supporting witnesses, primarily the Septuagint translation and the Dead Sea Scrolls, provide rich attestation prior to the Christian era.[3]

---

[2]Standard textbooks include B. M. Metzger, *The Text of the New Testament: Its Transmission, Corruption, and Restoration*, 2d ed. (New York: Oxford University Press, 1964), and Kurt Aland and Barbara Aland, *The Text of the New Testament: An Introduction to the Critical Editions and to the Theory and Practice of Modern Textual Criticism* (Grand Rapids: Eerdmans, 1987). For the latter, which is the most up-to-date and complete introduction, cf. my review in *WTJ* 50 (1988): 195–200; a second edition appeared in 1989.

[3]Cf. F. E. Deist, *Towards the Text of the Old Testament* (Pretoria: D. R. Church Booksellers, 1978); Ernst Würthwein, *The Text of the Old Testament: An*

Although we may therefore have full confidence in the integrity of the biblical text, there continue to be theoretical problems as well as specific questions that require attention. This book is hardly the place to provide instruction in such a difficult and specialized discipline, but the topic is of relevance to us insofar as it overlaps with more general linguistic issues.

We may, for example, apply the concepts of *noise* and *redundancy* to the transmission of texts.[4] When a textual error is introduced by a scribe, the message is distorted: noise (in the technical sense) has affected the transmission. Because of the inherent redundancy of language (and of writing in particular), the vast majority of these errors are self-correcting and do not affect the reader's perception of the message. Suppose we read a story in the newspaper that contains the following statement: *All four woman were hurt in tne accident.* If we are reading quickly, we may not even notice at all the two instances of noise in it: (1) the typesetter keyed the letter *a* rather than *e* in *women*; (2) the top of the letter *h* in *the* did not print out and so it looks like the letter *n*.

The reason we often fail to notice errors of this sort—even after laborious proofreading!—is that the message is perfectly clear from the context. Certainly the subject of the sentence must be plural, as the modifier *all four* and the verb *were* (both instances of redundancy) establish. As for the second error, there is no such word as *tne* in English; besides, the occurrence of *the* in such a context is highly predictable. Even if we notice the errors, of course, we will only be amused (or upset): we will not be misled into attributing a meaning to the sentence different from that intended by the writer. And if we happen to have pen in hand, we may be tempted to correct the errors. At that point, we are playing the role of textual critics. We are correcting "scribal errors" by means of the redundancy provided by the context.

As I have already pointed out, an exceedingly high

Introduction to the Biblia Hebraica (Grand Rapids: Eerdmans, 1979); E. Tov, *The Text-Critical Use of the Septuagint in Biblical Research*, Jerusalem Biblical Studies 3 (Jerusalem: Simor, 1981).

[4]See above, chap. 3, p. 56, and chap. 6, p. 108.

proportion of errors in biblical (or other) manuscripts are of this kind, and so the textual scholar need not think for longer than a second to determine what is the correct reading. There are, however, errors of various types. Note especially those errors introduced by scribes when they, consciously or unconsciously, were playing the role of textual critics themselves. It is fairly easy to demonstrate that, from time to time, copyists came across passages that did not "sound right" to them. They might notice an unexpected (i.e., not highly predictable) word, or a construction that seemed to them stylistically weak, or a statement that did not clearly fit their theological understanding of the topic at hand. If they thought that their master copy was in error, naturally they would alter the text toward greater redundancy.[5] Relying on the concept of entropy, Nida deals with such textual variations as follows:

> One might describe this process as a kind of semantic leveling in which unusual, difficult and complex expressions are changed into expressions which are easier to understand and more readily anticipated by a reader because they fit the context more neatly. They are "easier readings"—easier precisely because they are less specialized or unusual, hence having a greater degree of probability or predictability in relation to their contexts than do the "harder" or more unusual readings.[6]

It turns out, then, that the scholar is faced by two opposing tendencies (among others) that are operative in the process of textual transmission: the introduction of bad readings (i.e., noise, errors) and the creation of "improved" readings (in

[5] I must emphasize that these kinds of changes were not always the result of a conscious decision. A scribe may have been only vaguely aware of some unusual feature in the text; rather than taking the time to deliberate, he may have continued the writing process and semiconsciously adapted the text to a more commonplace construction. Some of the material in this section is taken from my article "Internal Evidence in the Text-Critical Use of the LXX," in *La Septuaginta en la investigación comtemporánea*, ed. N. Fernández Marcos (Madrid: C.S.I.C., 1985), pp. 151–67, esp. pp. 161–62.

[6] Eugene A. Nida, "The 'Harder Reading' in Textual Criticism: An Application of the Second Law of Thermodynamics," *BT* 32 (1981): 101–7, quotation from p. 105.

order to eliminate what the scribes perceived as noise but wasn't). Good textual critics, in other words, appreciate the conflict between *intrinsic probability* (Which of two or more variant readings makes the best contextual sense?) and *transcriptional probability* (Which reading was created by scribes because it may have made better sense *to them*?).[7] A good understanding of the character and function of language can help students of the Bible implement these principles in a responsible way.

Finally, it should be obvious that textual changes are not purely formal but semantic as well. As such, variant readings reflect broad interpretive frameworks and specific exegetical traditions. That is to say, textual transmission and exegetical history are closely related. Except for some rare instances when, say, Latin scribes may have mechanically copied Greek manuscripts they did not understand, the process of reading and interpretation was very much part of the scribes' activity. That is why even secondary readings that have no claim to represent the original text can nevertheless be of value to the interpreter.

Suppose, for example, that we notice some interesting readings introduced by the scribe of Papyrus 46 (or by the one who wrote his master copy?), such as his changing the phrase "the glory and praise of God" in Philippians 1:11 to "the glory of God and my praise"; or his adding to Philippians 3:12 the clause, "or have already been justified." We may well decide, in the process of *textual criticism*, that these variations are not original, but that is no reason to dismiss them in the process of *interpretation*.[8] Through variant readings scribes have passed on to us what they believed (rightly or wrongly) was the meaning of the text.

TRANSLATION

If scribes were involved in the difficult process of

---

[7]For a penetrating description of this problem, see the classic statement in B. F. Westcott and F. J. A. Hort, *The New Testament in the Original Greek*, 2 vols. (Graz, Austria: Akademische Druck- und Verlagsanstalt, 1974, orig. 1881) 2:26–27.

[8]Cf. my discussion in *Philippians*, pp. 63–64, 203–4; more generally, pp. 21–22.

interpretation (and communicating that interpretation) when they merely transcribed the text in the *same* language, what shall we say about those poor souls who seek to reproduce the message of Scripture in a different language? It is of course impossible (or at least unhelpful!) to translate a passage from language X into language Y unless one *knows* language X and *understands* what the original text says. Translators who view their work as pure renderings rather than interpretations only delude themselves; indeed, if they could achieve some kind of noninterpretative rendering, their work would be completely useless.

The task of producing a good translation is exceedingly arduous. Students of the biblical languages do not always have a good appreciation of what is involved. They have learned to produce "literal" translations by consulting the lexicon and so the process seems rather straightforward. In fact, however, a successful translation requires (1) mastery of the source language—certainly a much more sophisticated knowledge than one can acquire over a period of four or five years; (2) superb interpretive skills and breadth of knowledge so as not to miss the nuances of the original; and (3) a very high aptitude for writing in the target language so as to express accurately both the cognitive and the affective elements of the message.

Even when one has all that equipment, frustration lurks at every turn. If we capture with some precision the propositional content of a statement, we may give up the emotional nuances that form part of the total meaning. If we have a stroke of genius and come up with a turn of phrase that conveys powerfully the message of the original, we may realize that our rendering blurs somewhat its cognitive detail. Not surprisingly, some rabbis used to complain: "He who translates a verse literally is a liar, and he who paraphrases is a blasphemer!"[9] Italians are more concise: *traduttore traditore*, "translators are traitors."

---

[9]My own rendering of this saying is both literal and paraphrastic. See *The Babylonian Talmud*, Seder Nashim 8: Kiddushin, ed. I. Epstein (London: Soncino, 1936), p. 246 (= folio 49b): "R. Judah said: If one translates a verse literally, he is a liar; if he adds thereto, he is a blasphemer and a libeler."

The question of faithfulness in translation has become increasingly pressing in our time because of the very large number of available English versions of the Bible. What is a lay Christian to do when these versions differ from one another? Some of the differences are merely stylistic, as when one translator prefers the word *liberty* while another one uses *freedom*; most of us can live with that. A little more difficult to handle are differences that arise because the translators have used a different text base, as in Romans 5:1, where the NIV says, "we have peace with God," but the NEB renders, "let us continue at peace with God."[10] A third problem arises from differences in interpretation: KJV translates the first verb in John 5:39 as an imperative, "Search the Scriptures," while the NIV assumes it is an indicative, "You diligently study the Scriptures."[11]

The most fundamental difference, however, is that which pertains to philosophy of translation. We often speak of translations as being "literal" or "free." More precisely, some translations aim at representing the *form* of the original as closely as possible (without, however, doing violence to English grammar) while others, especially those influenced by linguistics, do not. It has become customary to describe the first approach as *formal correspondence* and the second as *dynamic equivalence*.[12] One seeks to achieve formal correspondence

---

[10]Two textual variants are involved. The first rendering reflects the indicative *echomen*, while the latter reflects the subjunctive *echōmen*.

[11]In contrast to the previous example, there is no textual variation here. The manuscripts are agreed in giving the verb *eraunate*, but this form can be analyzed as either indicative or imperative.

[12]A very influential work that propounds the method of dynamic equivalence is Eugene A. Nida, *Toward a Science of Translating: With Special Reference to Principles and Procedures Involved in Bible Translating* (Leiden: Brill, 1964). For a comprehensive textbook based on the ideas of Nida, John Beekman, and others, see Mildred L. Larson, *Meaning-Based Translation: A Guide to Cross-Language Equivalence* (Lanham, Md.: University Press of America, 1984). Among various important works from the Continent, see especially Wolfram Wilss, *The Science of Translation: Problems and Methods* (Tübinger Beiträge zur Linguistik 180; Tübingen: Gunter Narr, 1982), and the extensive manual by Valentín García Yebra, *Teoría y práctica de la traducción*, 2 vols. (Biblioteca románica hispánica 3/53; Madrid: Gredos, 1982). Literary scholars are often critical of the approach

primarily by the following means: (1) representing each word of the original with one word in English, as opposed to omitting or adding words; (2) establishing strict lexical equivalences, so that any given word in the original is rendered consistently with the corresponding English word throughout; and (3) retaining the word order of the original.

We may illustrate the differences with two translations produced by evangelical scholars. The NASB is the most widely used "literal" version, while the NIV adopts a moderate dynamic-equivalence approach. (1) If we read a narrative section of the Gospel of Mark in the NASB, we will notice that the word *and*, translating Greek *kai*, is used with high frequency. Because such repetition is not characteristic of written English narrative, the NIV simply omits most of these occurrences. (2) In the NASB the word *flesh* occurs quite a few times in Galatians as the standard equivalent for Greek *sarx*, whereas the NIV renders the word in the following ways:

"man" (1:16, lit. "flesh and blood")
"no one" (2:16, lit. "all flesh not")
"human effort" (3:3)
"illness" (4:13, lit. "weakness of the flesh")
"in the ordinary way" (4:23, lit. "according to the flesh")
"sinful nature" (5:13-24)
"outwardly" (6:12, lit. "in the flesh")
"flesh" (6:13!)

Finally, (3) notice how the complex sentence structure of Hebrews 7:20-22 is followed closely by the NASB:

> And inasmuch as *it was* not without an oath (for they indeed became priests without an oath, but He with an oath through the One who said to Him,

taken by linguists because the latter allegedly see translation as merely the transmission of data rather than as the process of literary creation. See especially L. G. Kelly, *The True Interpreter: A History of Translation Theory and Practice in the West* (New York: St. Martin's, 1979), and Stephen Prickett, *Words and* The Word: *Language, Poetics and Biblical Interpretation* (Cambridge: Cambridge University Press, 1986). For a more explicitly theological critique of dynamic equivalence, see Jakob van Bruggen, *The Future of the Bible* (Nashville: Thomas Nelson, 1978), chap. 4.

"The Lord has sworn,
And will not change His mind,
'Thou art a priest forever'");
so much the more also Jesus has become the guarantee of a
better covenant.

The NIV, on the other hand, renders the sentence with more
idiomatic English by breaking it up into smaller ones:

And it was not without an oath! Others became priests without
any oath, but he became a priest with an oath when God said to
him:
"The Lord has sworn
and will not change his mind:
You are a priest forever.' "
Because of this oath, Jesus has become the guarantee of a
better covenant.

In fact, no translation is fully consistent in implementing
its approach. Some years ago I was asked to review a "literal"
Spanish version of Isaiah, and I did so by comparing it to
another Spanish version fully committed to the principle of
dynamic equivalence. It was surprising, and amusing, to notice
a significant number of passages where the former version
avoided a literal rendering (perhaps because the Hebrew idiom
sounded strange) while the latter translated literally (perhaps
because of the literary quaintness of the original)! Differences in
translation philosophy have produced much debate, some of it
highly emotional, and this book is not the place to solve the
controversy, but readers may find it worthwhile to note the
following points.

The principle of dynamic equivalence is widely favored by
professional linguists, and so it has become common to
denounce versions such as the NASB as linguistically naïve and
inadequate. From the other side, it is just as common to hear
complaints that the dynamic-equivalence approach reflects a
low view of the authority of Scripture. Both of these complaints suffer from the slur factor, both are misleading, and they
both tend to polarize parties unnecessarily.

We must ever keep in mind that no one translation can
possibly convey fully and unambiguously the meaning of the

original. Different translators, and even different philosophies of translation, contribute to express various features of the original. If we isolate some of the passages from Galatians quoted above, the NIV renderings do convey more faithfully to the English reader the point of Paul's statements than does the literal translation, "flesh." On the other hand, there is a conceptual connection among some of those uses of the Greek *sarx*; such a connection is part of the total meaning expressed by Paul, and the NASB reader is much more likely to capture it.[13]

Moreover, recent advances in linguistics place much emphasis on the context of speech. The admirable desire to produce translations that *do not sound like translations* and are thus clearer and more accessible to the modern reader must be accompanied by the reminder that the biblical stories took place in the Middle East rather than the Western world, in ancient times rather than in the twentieth century. To the extent that "readable" translations indirectly encourage modern readers to forget such a setting, to that extent they also fail to capture part of the meaning of the text.[14] Besides, one detects a definite tendency to make modern translations much simpler than the original Greek and Hebrew. If the Corinthians had some difficulty understanding Paul's Greek, it is no disgrace when a modern English reader has to struggle through a long apostolic sentence.

It is also misleading, however, to assume that a rendering that is *formally* equivalent to the original necessarily conveys the meaning more faithfully. If I translate the Spanish sentence

---

[13]Cf. also Edward L. Greenstein, *Essays on Biblical Method and Translation* (BJS 92; Atlanta: Scholars Press, 1989), p. 87, who complains that the *Good News Bible*, by translating Hebrew *bayit* in 2 Samuel 7 with three different English words ("palace," "temple," "dynasty"), "completely [obliterates] the thematic connections of the original," that is, the royal house of David, the temporary house where God dwelt, and the dynastic house that God promised to David.

[14]Prickett goes so far as to suggest that "those who see translation essentially in terms of data-transmission" (i.e., linguists) are the ones "who turn most readily to paraphrase, while those who think in interpretative terms tend to cling more faithfully to the actual words of the original text. Literal translation is a form of hermeneutics" (*Words*, p. 29). Cf. also my comments in *Has the Church Misread the Bible?* pp. 50–51.

Tengo frío en los pies literally, "I have cold in the feet," rather than idiomatically, "My feet are cold," English readers will probably understand the rendering, but they will gain absolutely nothing by its literalness—indeed, they could be misled to think that there is some special nuance they are missing! Literal translations are easier to produce, and the approach can degenerate into an excuse for not doing the hard exegetical and literary work of conveying faithfully the meaning of the ancient text to the modern reader.

TEACHING

What a scribe does imperceptibly when transcribing a manuscript, and what a translator does behind the scenes when translating a biblical book—that is what a teacher does explicitly when passing on the meaning of the text to someone else. There is a long, unbroken process of linguistic transmission that reaches a climax when the gospel message is proclaimed today.

The effort we spend on interpreting the Bible cannot end with our personal enjoyment. We learn so that we may teach (cf. Heb. 5:12). We receive so that we may give. The serious study of human language helps us to understand the divine word. May we faithfully use that language to communicate to others the message of grace.

APPENDIX

THE BIBLICAL LANGUAGES IN THEOLOGICAL EDUCATION

From time to time a few of my Greek students, upon hearing my point of view, work up the courage to ask me what probably all of them are thinking: What then is the point of learning the biblical languages? Some readers of this book may be asking themselves the same question.

A few years ago, when our seminary was conducting one of its recruiting conferences, I was asked to address the prospective students on the value of studying Greek. Suspecting that some of these students were already looking forward to the possibility of accomplishing great feats of exegetical prestidigitation, I began by giving a list of *bad* reasons for studying the biblical languages. Unfortunately, my time was limited and I ended up with only a few minutes to expound on the good reasons. Some weeks later a colleague reported to me that one of those students had decided not to come to our seminary. Evidently I had convinced him that there was no point in attending an institution that had such hefty language requirements! I have not been asked to give my talk again.

During the past few generations, teachers of New Testament Greek—particularly in conservative American institutions—have been inclined, in the interest of encouraging their students, to overemphasize the *direct* value of Greek grammar for exegesis and theology. As a colleague in another institution has remarked, the process of "demythologizing" the value of the biblical languages has created the need for a valid justification of the traditional seminary requirement. Indeed, not a few

141

seminaries have weakened or altogether abandoned such language requirements. While I have no intentions in this brief appendix to provide a full rationale for the study of biblical languages, readers of this book deserve at least a few comments regarding this important issue.

We should note at the outset that there are two distinct questions before us. One has a strictly personal character: Why should an *individual* preparing for ministry study the biblical languages? The second question has wider implications: Why should a *theological seminary* require the study of the biblical languages? Of course, these two issues are closely related: presumably, no seminary would require the languages if they were of no value at all to individuals. Nevertheless, the questions are distinct and may require somewhat different answers.

I do not hesitate to acknowledge that, in some situations, it may be possible for pastors, as well as others engaged in more general kinds of Christian ministry, to do their jobs without solid training in the biblical languages. Many of the early Latin fathers—notably Augustine—had only a smattering of Greek and knew virtually no Hebrew, yet they appear to have managed respectably well! But that is hardly a conclusive argument against language requirements. Augustine also had no formal training in modern counseling and other areas of practical theology, yet most of us would consider that fact somewhat irrelevant in determining curricular requirements.

Today we are far removed from the cultural and linguistic world of the Bible. It is an illusion for us to think that we can understand the biblical text while ignoring the distance—both temporal and geographic—that separates us from that text. Someone has to bridge the gap. Translations act as our primary bridges. Individual translators have done the hard work necessary to make the ancient text accessible to the modern believer. It could be said that ministers who have not studied the biblical languages enslave themselves to English translations. To be sure, this need not be an absolutely fatal relationship, but it certainly puts ministers at a serious disadvantage.

Suppose, for example, that a parishioner notices a significant difference between two New Testament translations. On what grounds will the "Greekless" pastor offer a responsible solution? Again, while we are blessed with a multitude of fine commentaries, they can prove to be almost useless if we cannot follow the linguistic arguments involved. The problem becomes critical if the pastor has a well-educated congregation—and even more so if some of the members are college students who find themselves bombarded by the arguments of unbelieving professors. Inability by the pastor to provide reasonable responses to pressing questions can prove destructive in some sensitive situations.

It may be worthwhile to keep in mind that, more often than not, grammar has a negative yet important function: grammatical knowledge may not directly result in a sensational new truth, but it may play a key role in *preventing* interpretive mistakes. Take, for instance, the doctrine of Christ's deity. It would *not* be quite accurate to say that Greek syntax directly proves this doctrine. It is certainly true, however, that it can *disprove* certain heretical ideas. For example, proponents of some cults are fond of pointing out that the last reference to God in John 1:1 does not include the definite article and so should be translated "a god" or "divine." Someone with little or no knowledge of Greek could easily be persuaded by this argument. A reasonably good understanding of predicate clauses in Greek, however, is all one needs to demonstrate that the argument has no foundation whatever (the article that accompanies the predicate noun is routinely dropped to distinguish the predicate from the subject of the clause—besides, there are numerous and indisputable references to God, as in verses 6, 13, and 18 of the same chapter, that do not include the article).

Quite possibly, however, the most significant benefit of acquiring a knowledge of the biblical languages is intangible. Most of us are conditioned to think that nothing is truly valuable that does not have an immediate and concrete payoff, but a little reflection dispels that illusion. Consider the teaching we all received from birth. Has most of it been *immediately* rewarding? We are simply not conscious of how deeply we have been molded by countless experiences that affect our perspective, our thinking, our decisions. Similarly, a measure of proficiency in the biblical languages provides the framework that promotes responsibility in the handling of the text. Continued exposure to the original text expands our horizon and furnishes us with a fresh and more authentic perspective than that which we bring from our modern, English-speaking situation.

In my own preaching during the past twenty-five years, explicit references to Greek and Hebrew have become less and less frequent. But that hardly means I have paid less attention to the languages or that they have become less significant in my work of interpretation. Quite the contrary. It's just that coming up with those rich "exegetical nuggets" is not necessarily where the real, substantial payoff lies.

There is, however, a whole different set of reasons that we ought to appeal to in favor of a strong biblical language requirement in seminary training. That is, even if we were to decide that many *individual* ministers have in fact little use for Greek and Hebrew, there are some powerful considerations that come to bear when we focus attention on the larger, *corporate* responsibilities of theological institutions. In a nutshell: Relaxing the language requirements inevitably lowers the quality of instruction and adversely affects biblical scholarship.

No doubt, it will be argued by some that as long as the languages continue to be offered as electives, students interested in the subject can be trained. But that makes about as much sense as saying that algebra and history should merely be electives in the high schools. As the argument goes: How often does the typical graduate make use of algebraic equations and historical dates in his or her day-to-day work? Among various responses to such a question, I am interested in pointing out, first, that such an elective system would necessarily weaken the intellectual character of the whole school by lowering its cultural literacy; and second, that potentially brilliant scholars in math and history might never have an opportunity to develop an interest in those subjects.

It should go without saying that if a professor in biblical studies is unable to deal with technical linguistic arguments in a class because most of the students have not taken Greek and Hebrew, the level of instruction necessarily drops. Moreover, the important education that takes place as students converse with one another also plummets several notches. The natural tendency to gravitate toward "relevancy" and pragmatism can do nothing but flourish in such an environment. And the end result is an increase in the poisonous anti-intellectualism that has already taken its toll in the evangelical church.

But I fear most of all for the future of biblical scholarship. Many are the students who have acknowledged that, if they had not been forced to take Greek and Hebrew, they would not have done so, thus missing what they now consider a foundational element in their theological education. Dropping the language requirement leads inexorably to a drain in the pool of potential scholars. Can we afford to abandon the scientific study of the Bible and leave it in the hands of those who have no regard for its authority?

These considerations have a special significance in the context of today's hermeneutical debates. We would all like to find shortcuts that may lead us to the right answers without the hard, and sometimes tedious, work of responsible biblical exegesis. But the shortcuts simply do not exist. May we be given the tenacity to do whatever needs to be done to advance the church's understanding of God's infallible Word.

FOR FURTHER READING

A complete list of works cited may be found in the index of modern authors and titles. In this section I have included only a few helpful works.

Cambridge University Press has produced numerous works in the area of linguistics. At a popular level notice especially David Crystal, *The Cambridge Encyclopedia of Language* (1987), a clear and profusely illustrated work covering virtually every field related to the study of language. The four-volume work *Linguistics: The Cambridge Survey*, ed. Frederick J. Newmeyer (1988) is an unusually successful anthology in which each contributor has sought to describe the state of the art in modern linguistics. Although this work presupposes some knowledge of the field, most of the articles avoid highly technical language and are therefore accessible to a wide range of readers. In addition, the series Cambridge Textbooks in Linguistics offers full-length, intermediate-level volumes on almost every subdiscipline, such as phonology, morphology, dialectology, historical linguistics, and the like.

On the application of linguistics to biblical studies, see the Annotated Bibliography in M. Silva, *Biblical Words and Their Meaning: An Introduction to Lexical Semantics* (Grand Rapids: Zondervan, 1983), pp. 180–82. Recent publications in this field include David A. Black, *Linguistics for Students of New Testament Greek: A Survey of Basic Concepts and Applications* (Grand Rapids: Baker, 1988), and Peter Cotterell and Max Turner, *Linguistics and Biblical Interpretation* (Downers Grove, Ill.: InterVarsity, 1989); cf. my review of the latter in *WTJ* 51 (1989): 389–90. Of special significance is the forthcoming volume by J. P. Louw and E. A. Nida, *Lexical Semantics of the Greek New Testament*.

The reader should also refer to the footnotes in relevant sections of the present book, especially pages 112 (verbal aspect), 119 (discourse analysis), and 135 (translation).

INDEX OF MODERN AUTHORS AND TITLES

(Full bibliographical information may be found in the first reference to individual works. Virtually all the page references are to the footnotes.)

INDEX OF SUBJECTS

(This index includes selected Greek, Hebrew, and Aramaic words.)

INDEX OF BIBLICAL PASSAGES

159